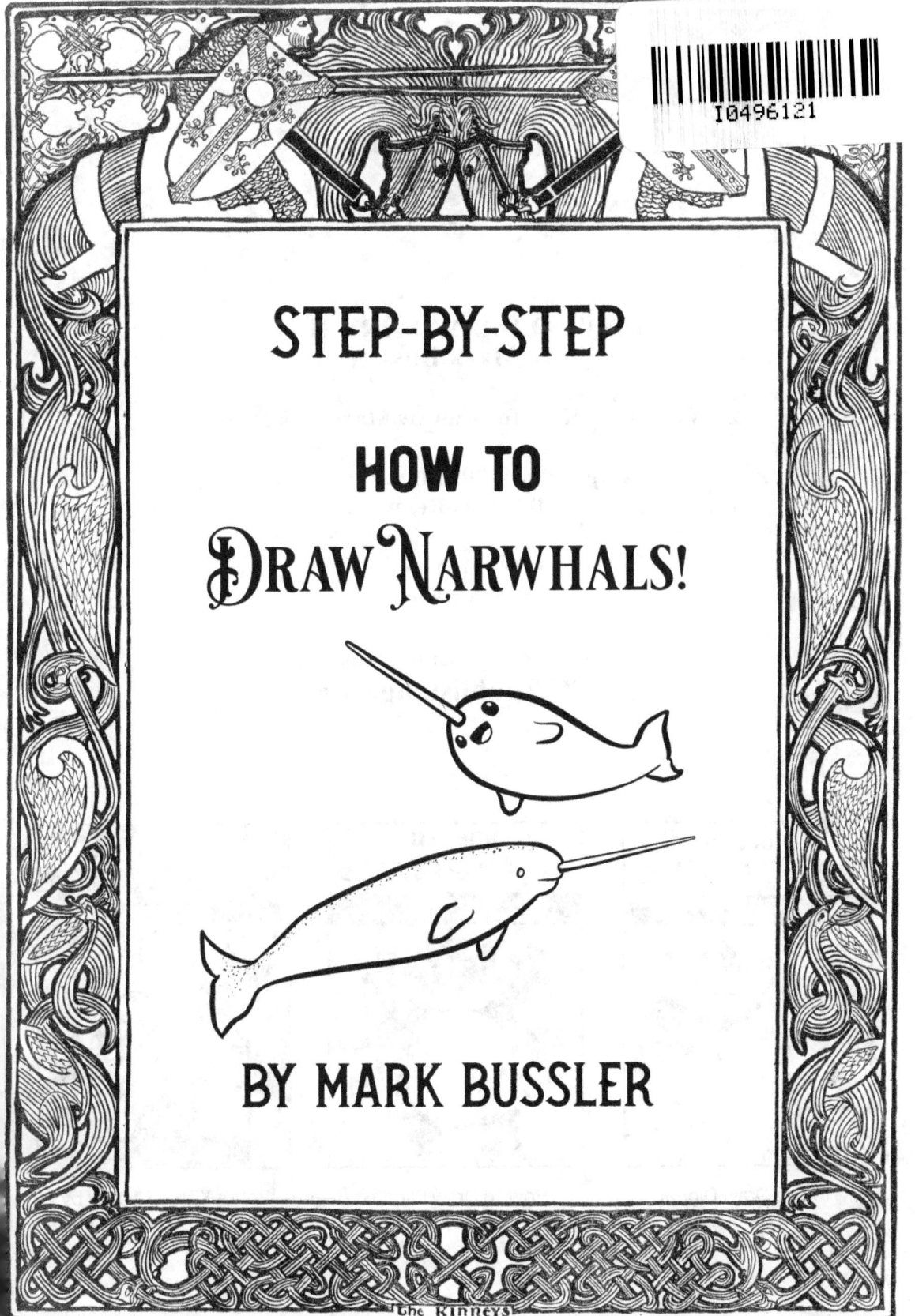

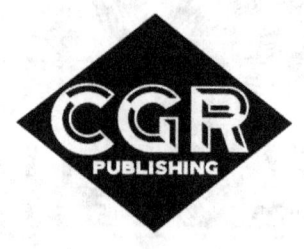

HOW TO DRAW NARWHALS
by Mark Bussler

Book 3 in the How To Draw by Mark Bussler series

Copyright © 2020 Inecom, LLC.
All Rights Reserved

Cover Design by
Mark Bussler

More How-To-Draw Books At
CGRpublishing.com

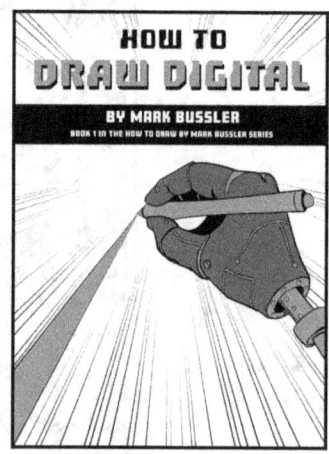

How To Draw Digital
by Mark Bussler

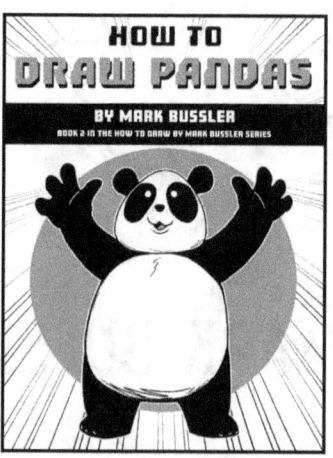

How To Draw Pandas
by Mark Bussler

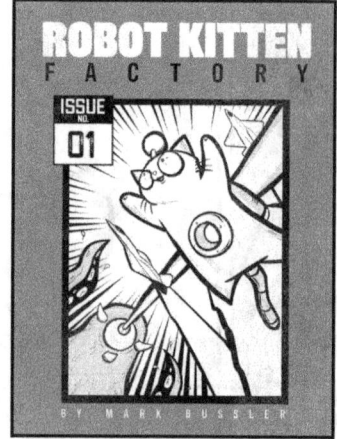

Robot Kitten Factory by
Mark Bussler

TABLE OF CONTENTS

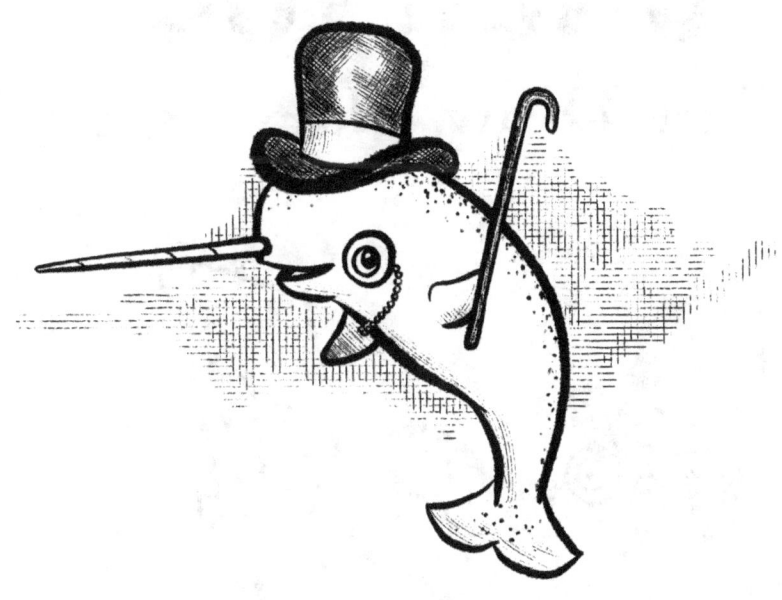

Introduction - 5
Artist's Tools - 8
What is a Narwhal? - 10
Artistic License - 14
Sum of its Parts - 16
Proportions - 20
Step-By-Step - 22
Kawaii Narwhal - 30
Realistic Narwhal - 40
Advanced Tips - 47
Get Creative - 50
Sketch Practice - 56

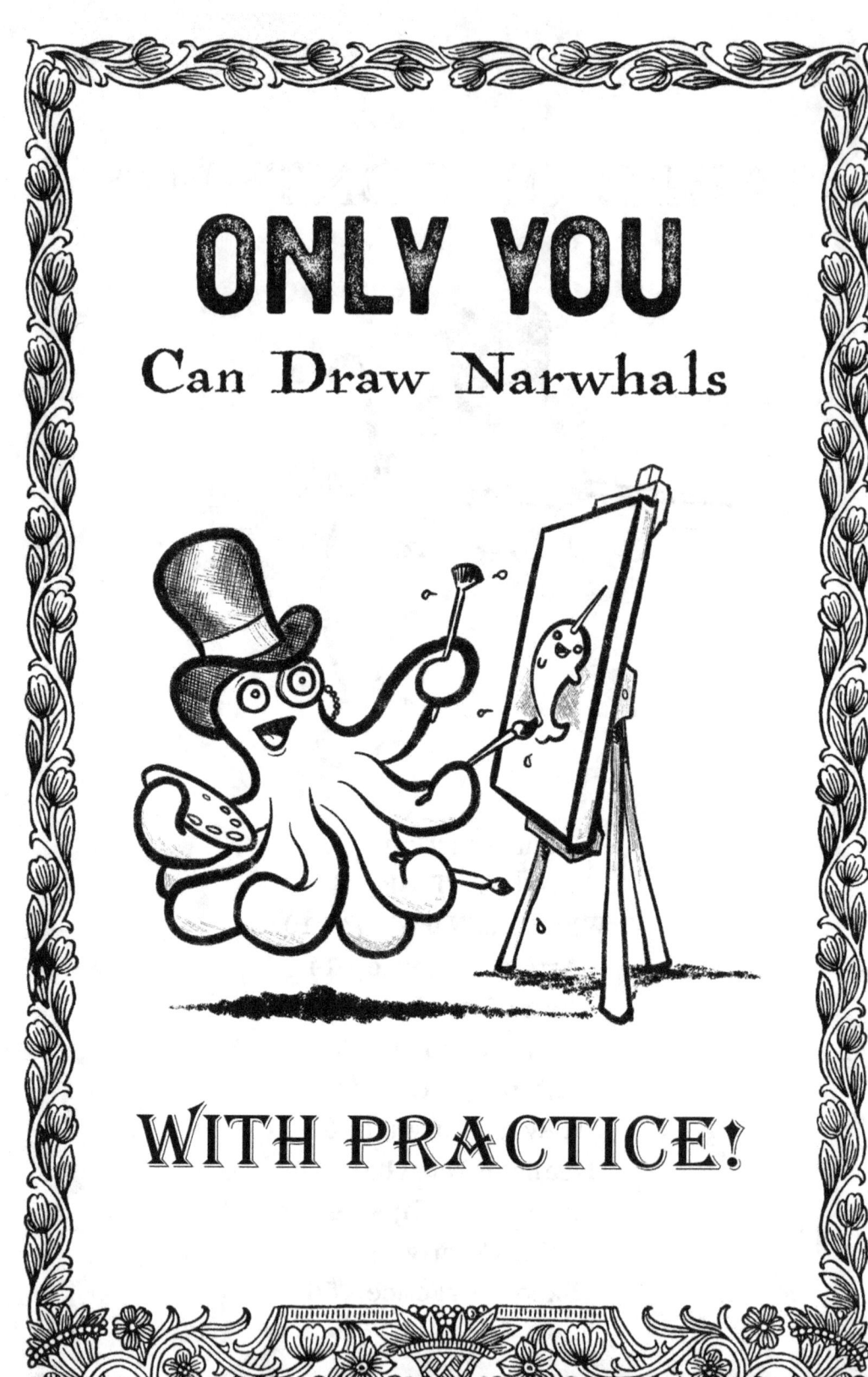

INTRODUCTION

Hello! I'm **The Horrible Octopus**, and I'll be your guide through the wonderful world of drawing realistic and kawaii narwhals using fun step-by-step techniques that build upon basic geometric shapes.

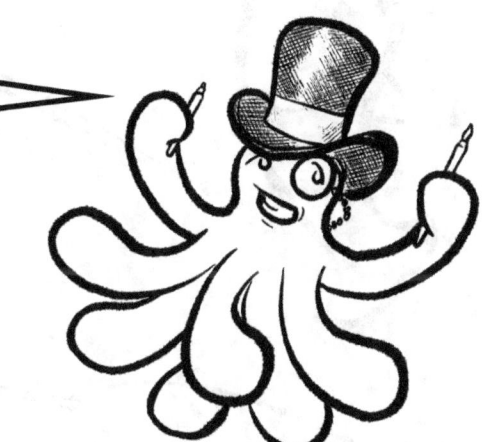

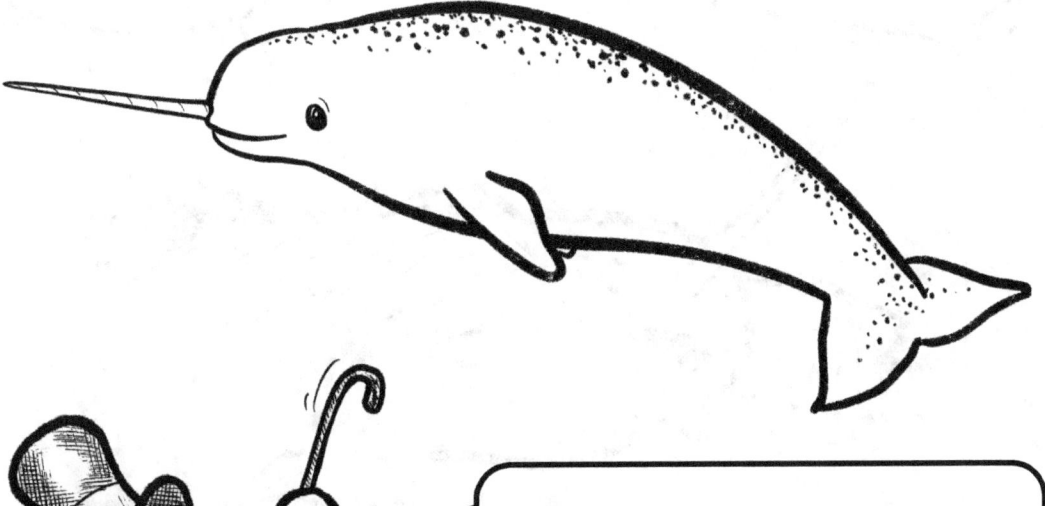

Soon you'll be able to draw this narwhal, and many like it, by combining three easy to draw shapes with a bit of imagination and lots of practice.

Remember, narwhals are awesome. You need to draw narwhals because they can't draw themselves (unless they're really talented narwhals.)

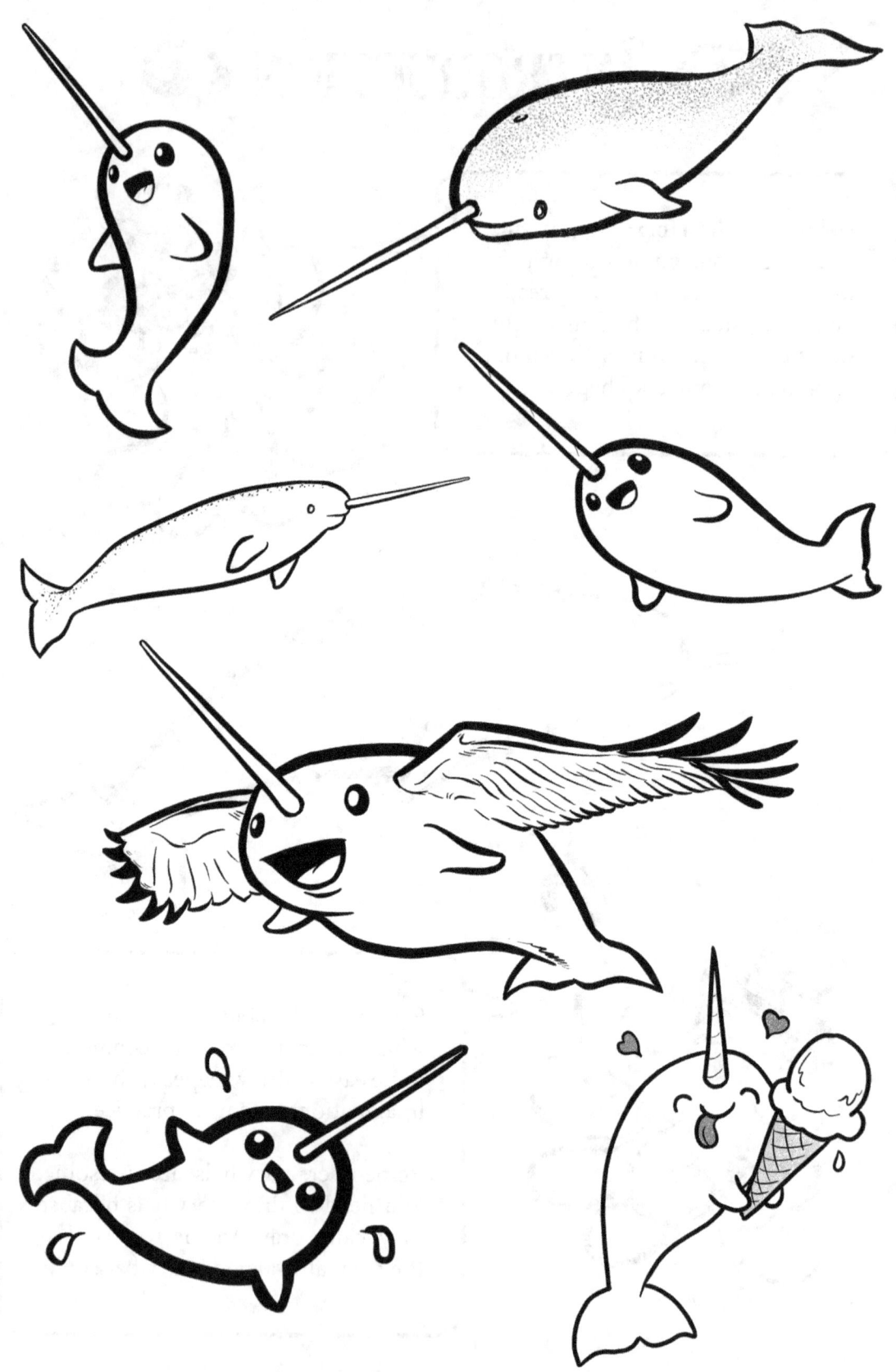

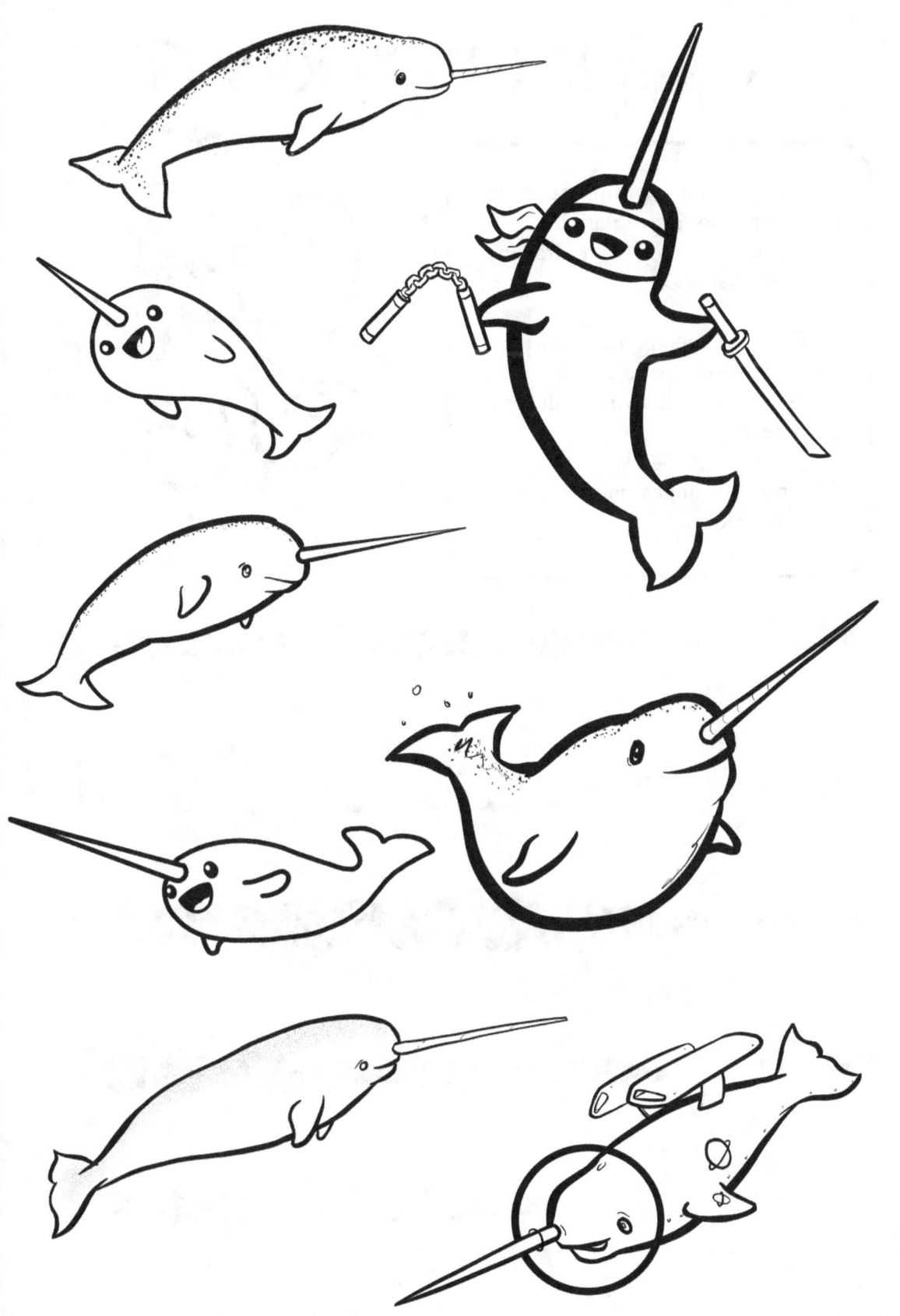

Artist's Tools

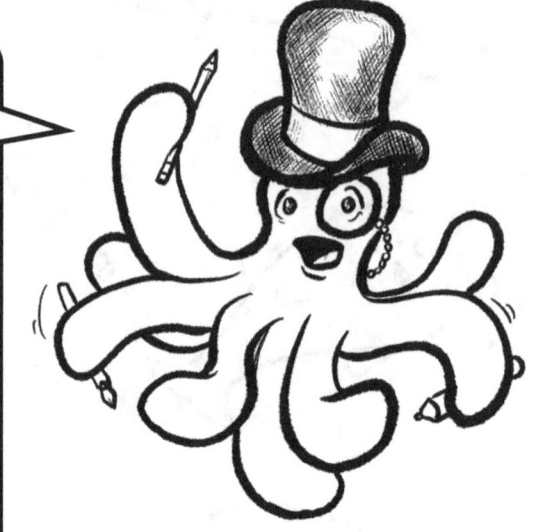

You don't need anything fancy to learn how to draw narwhals. In fact, the less fancy your drawing tools, the better!

Grab some paper, pencils, markers, pens, crayons, chalk, finger paint, or even a digital drawing tablet and prepare to get creative.

(Do not use finger paint on your parent's iPad!)

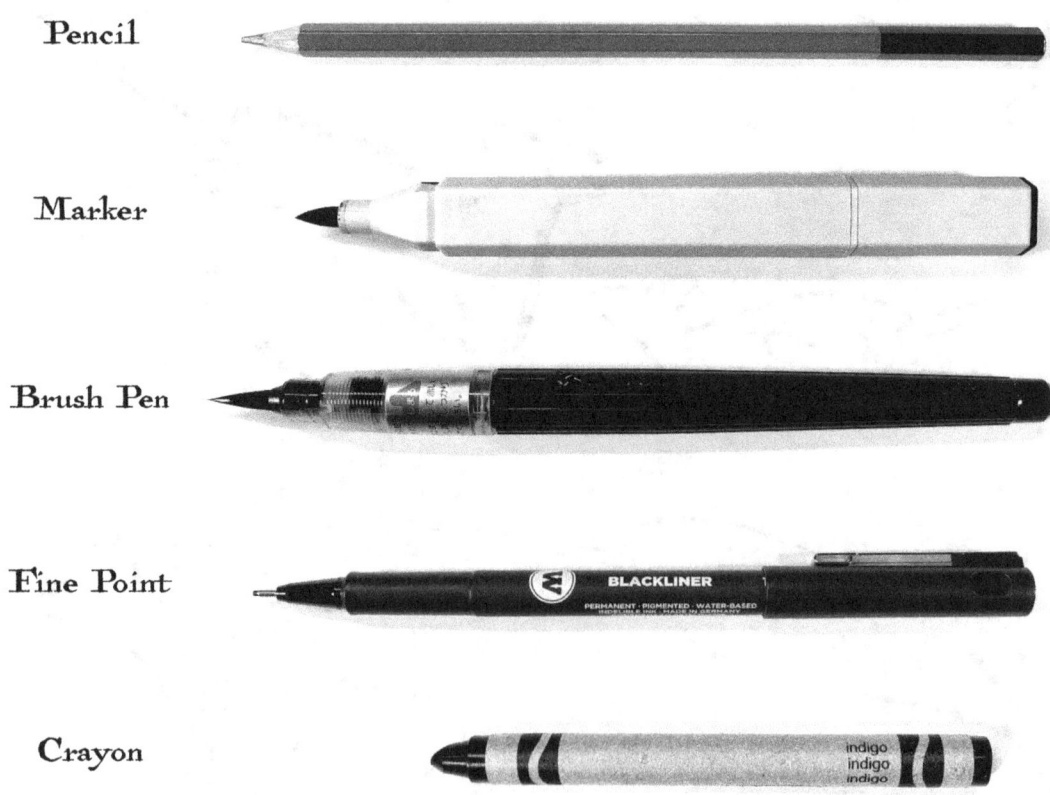

Pencil

Marker

Brush Pen

Fine Point

Crayon

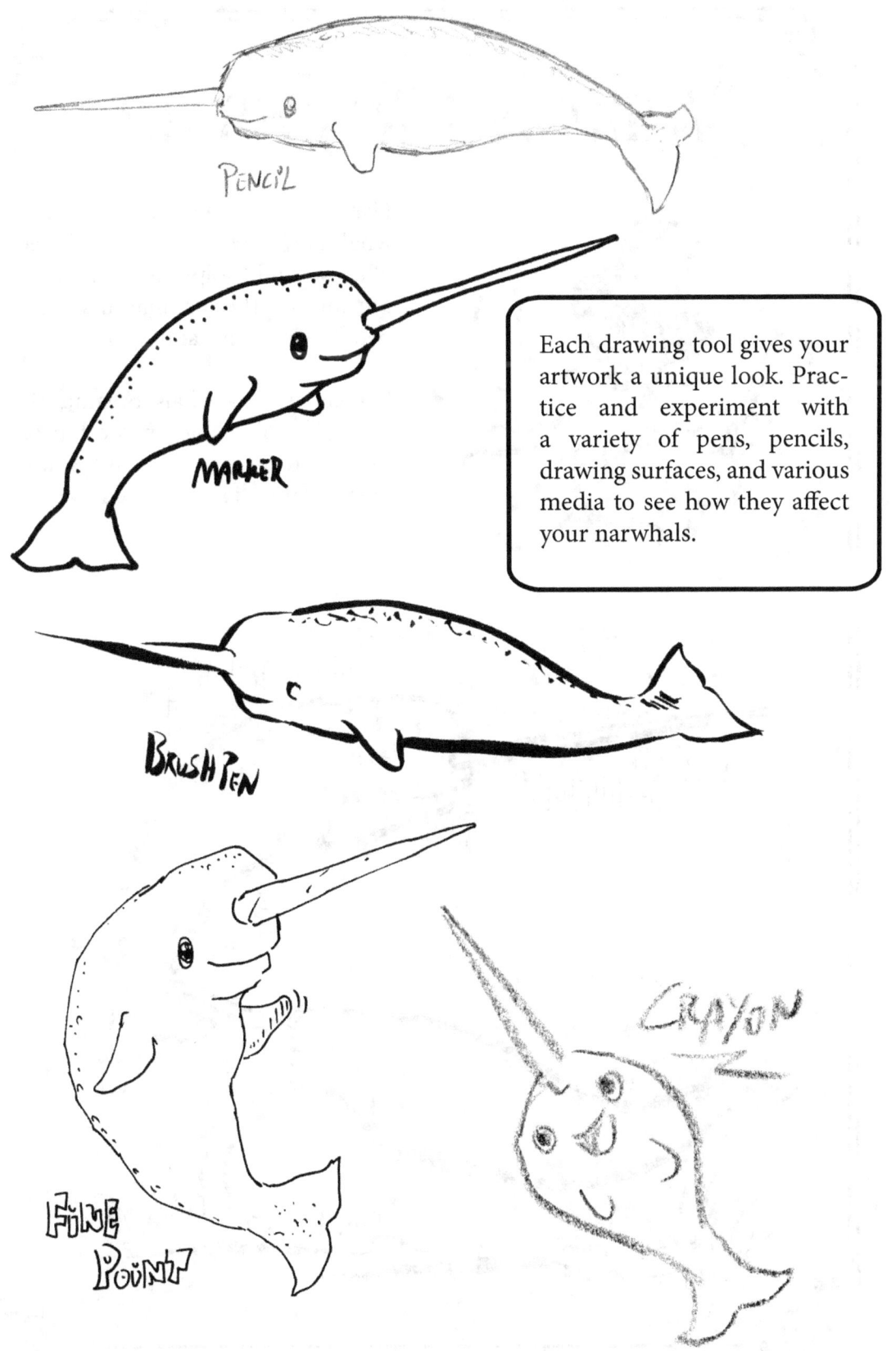

Each drawing tool gives your artwork a unique look. Practice and experiment with a variety of pens, pencils, drawing surfaces, and various media to see how they affect your narwhals.

What is a Narwhal?

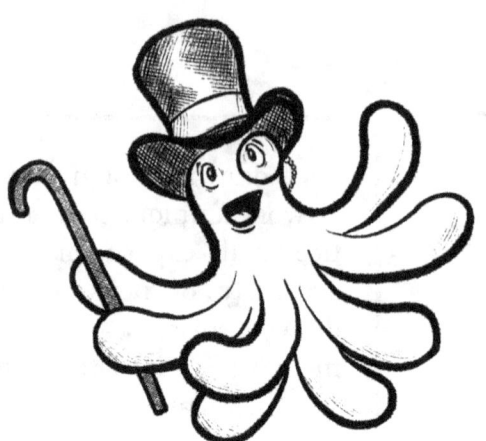

Narwhals are whales like blue whales, humpback whales, killer whales, and dolphins. Narwhals are not fish. They are mammals like people, elephants, and tigers.

Unlike fish, narwhals breathe air through a blowhole on the top of their head and have tail fins that are horizontally aligned to their body.

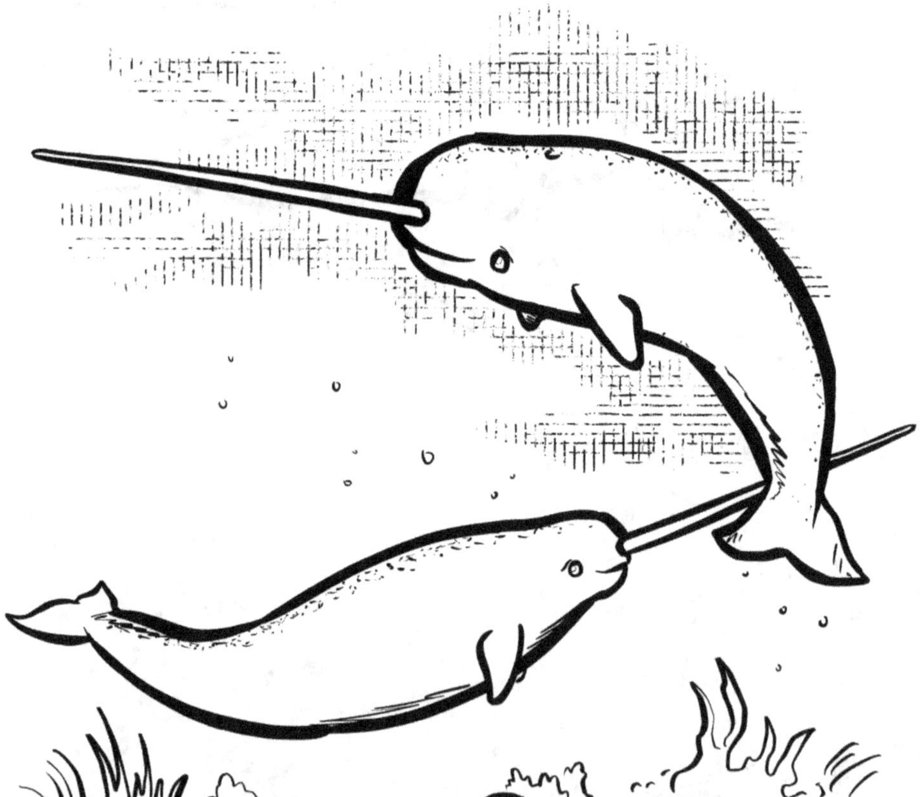

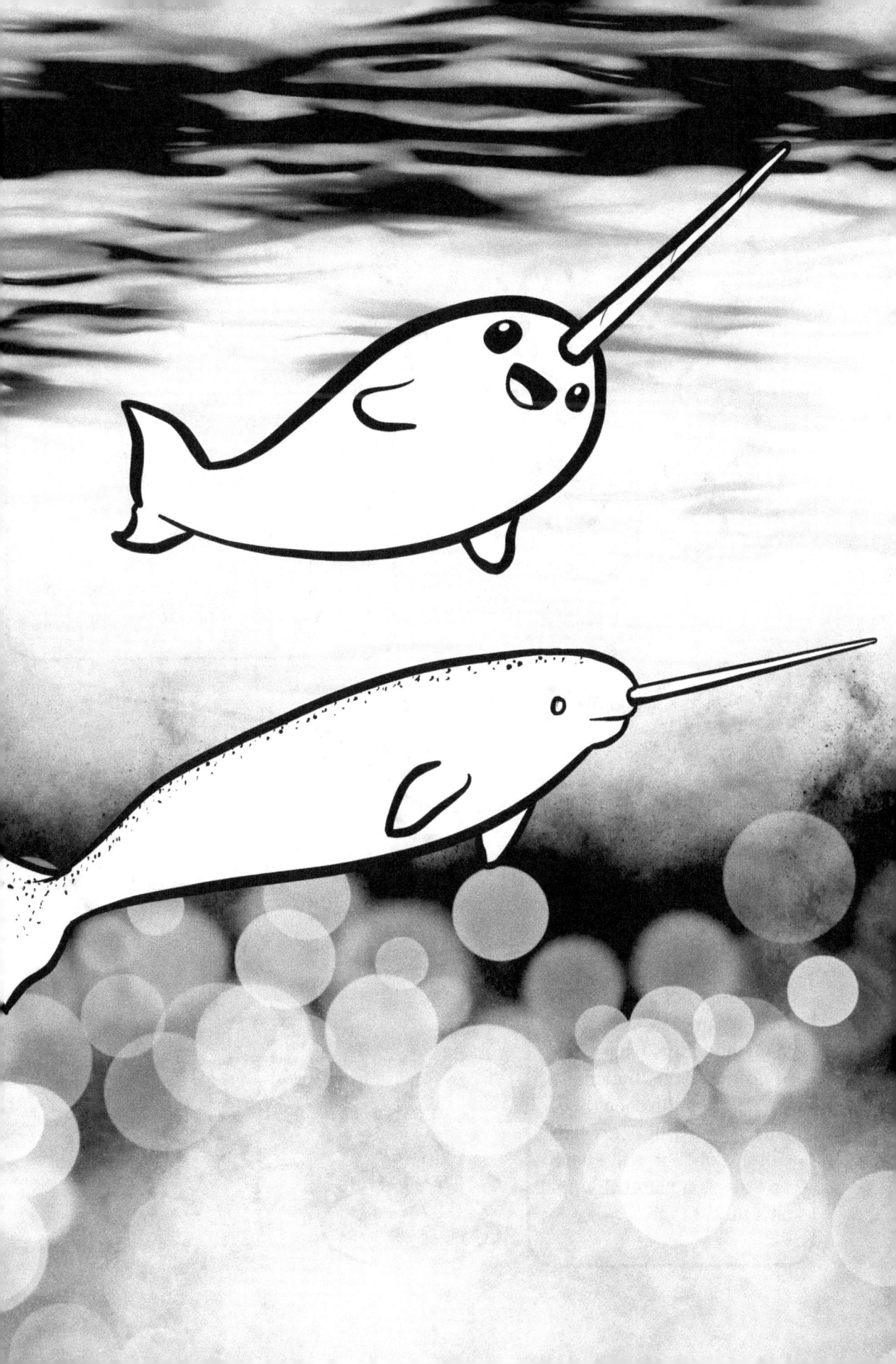

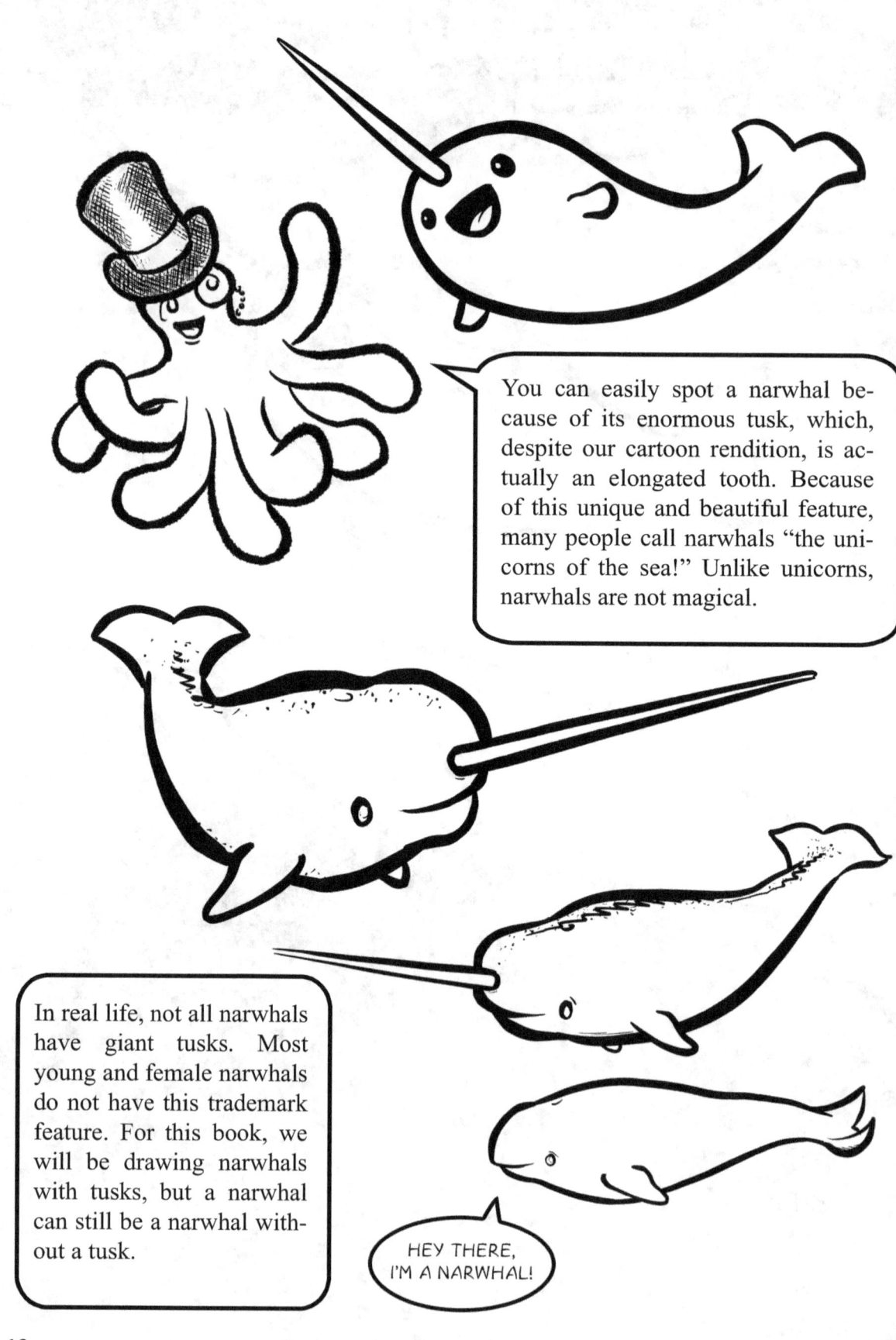

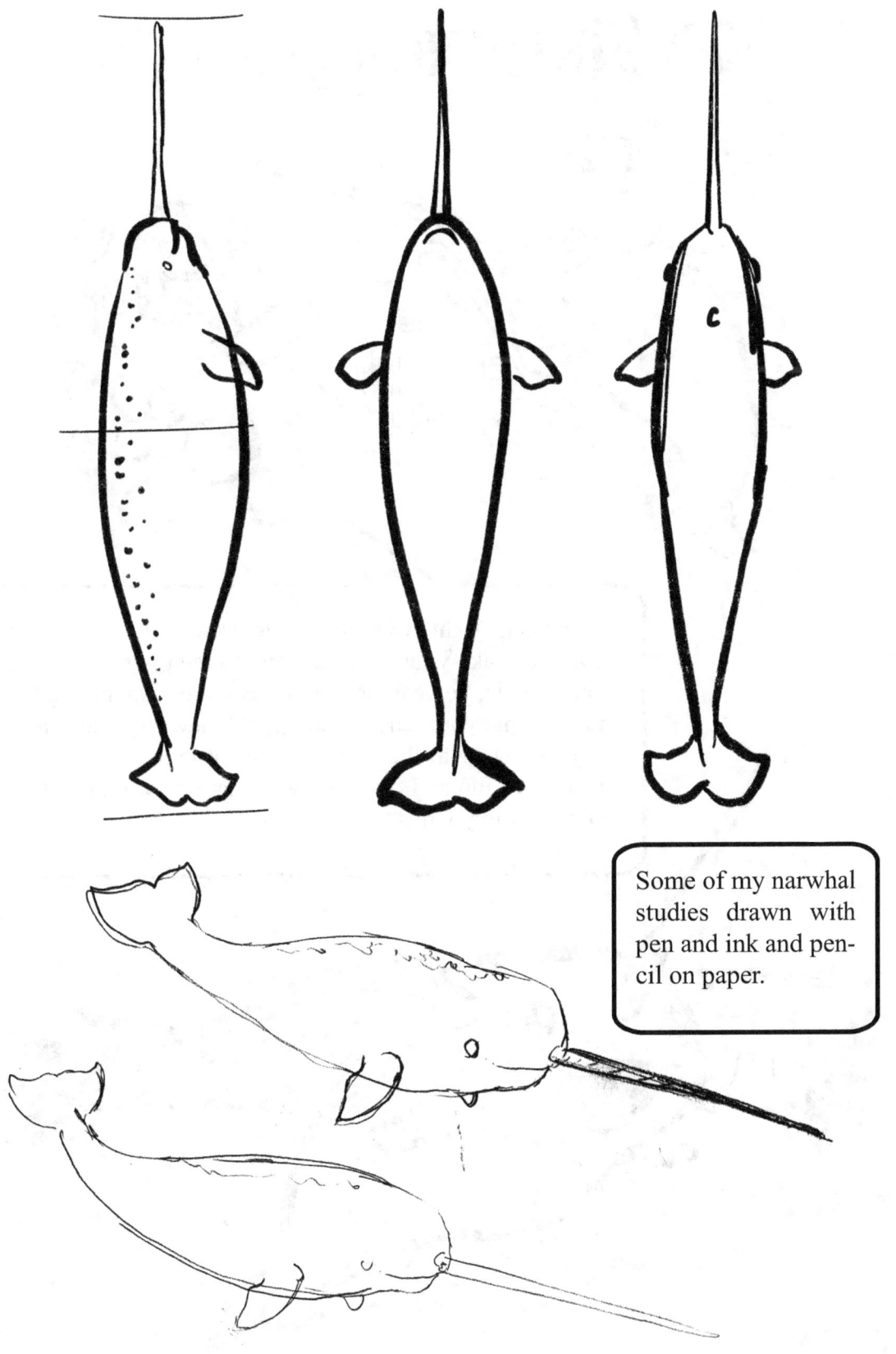

Some of my narwhal studies drawn with pen and ink and pencil on paper.

Artistic License

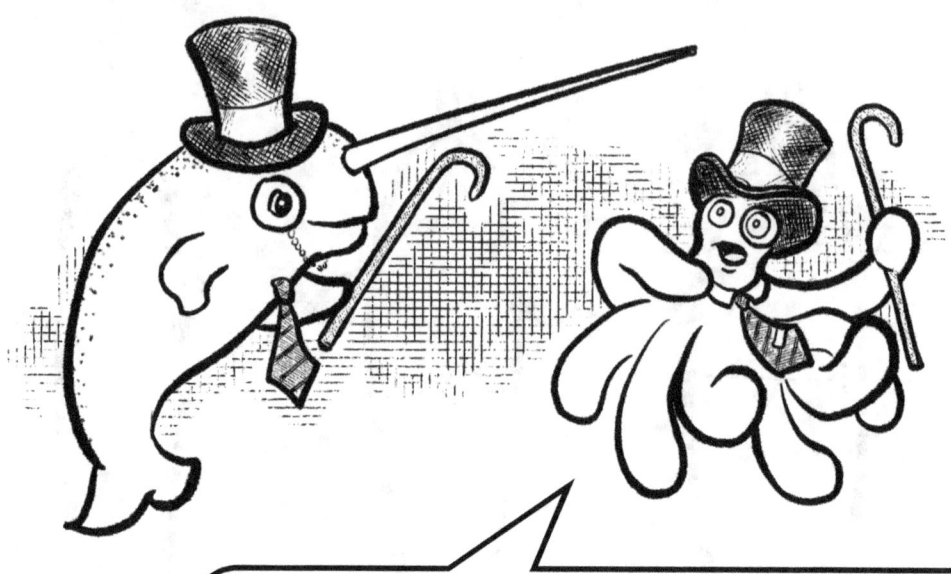

There is no right or wrong way to draw a narwhal. If you want to make your narwhal bright green with a top hat and necktie, you can do that. I recommend including the tusk so that your readers can quickly identify it as a narwhal (even with the monocle.) What is most important is to have fun and draw the way that you want to. How about adding wings?

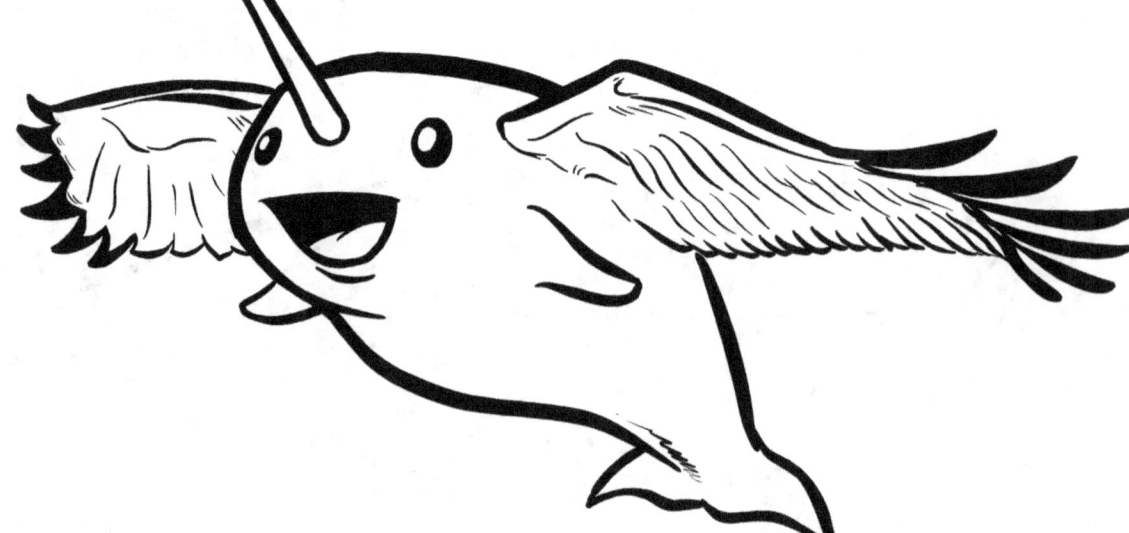

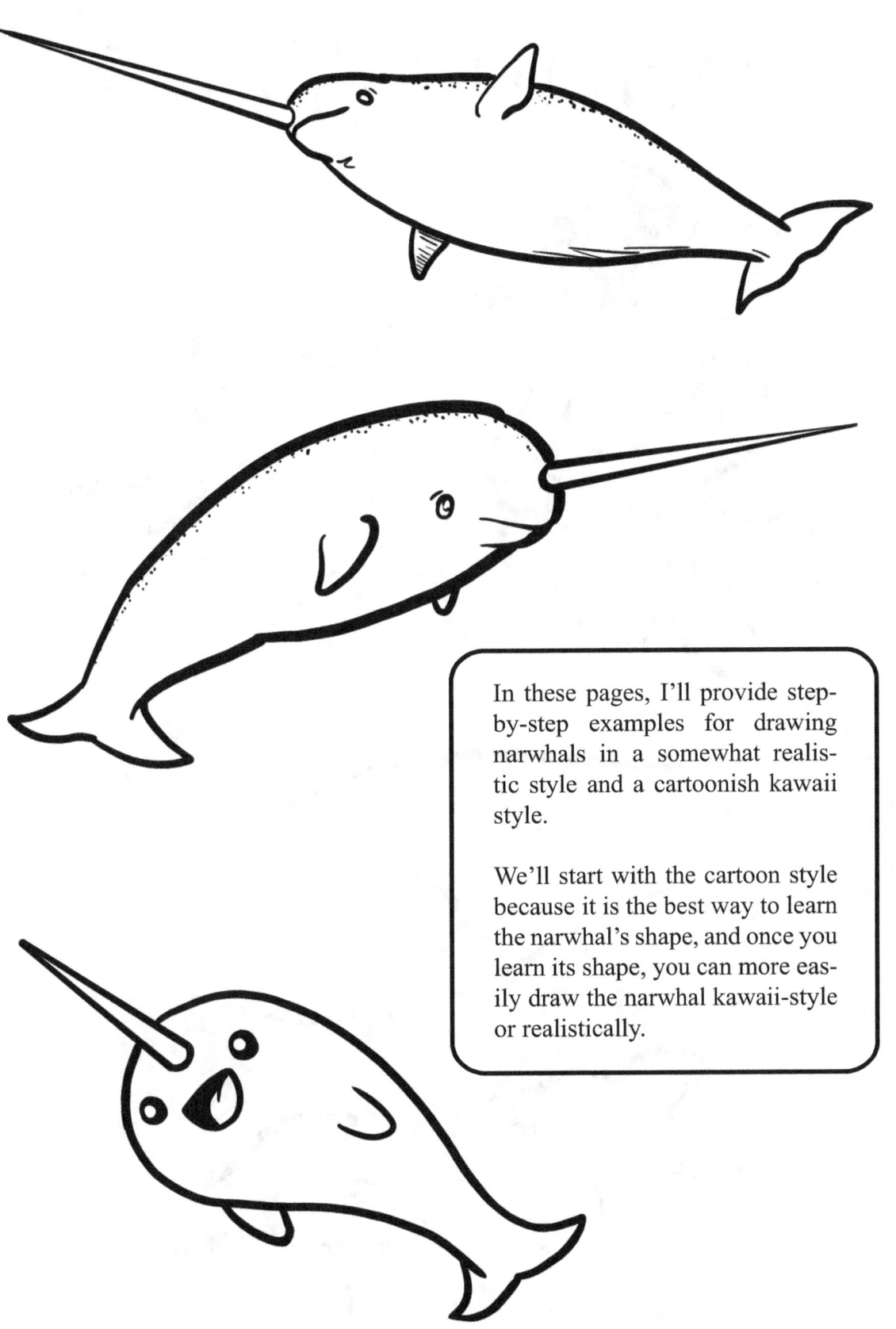

In these pages, I'll provide step-by-step examples for drawing narwhals in a somewhat realistic style and a cartoonish kawaii style.

We'll start with the cartoon style because it is the best way to learn the narwhal's shape, and once you learn its shape, you can more easily draw the narwhal kawaii-style or realistically.

Sum of its Parts

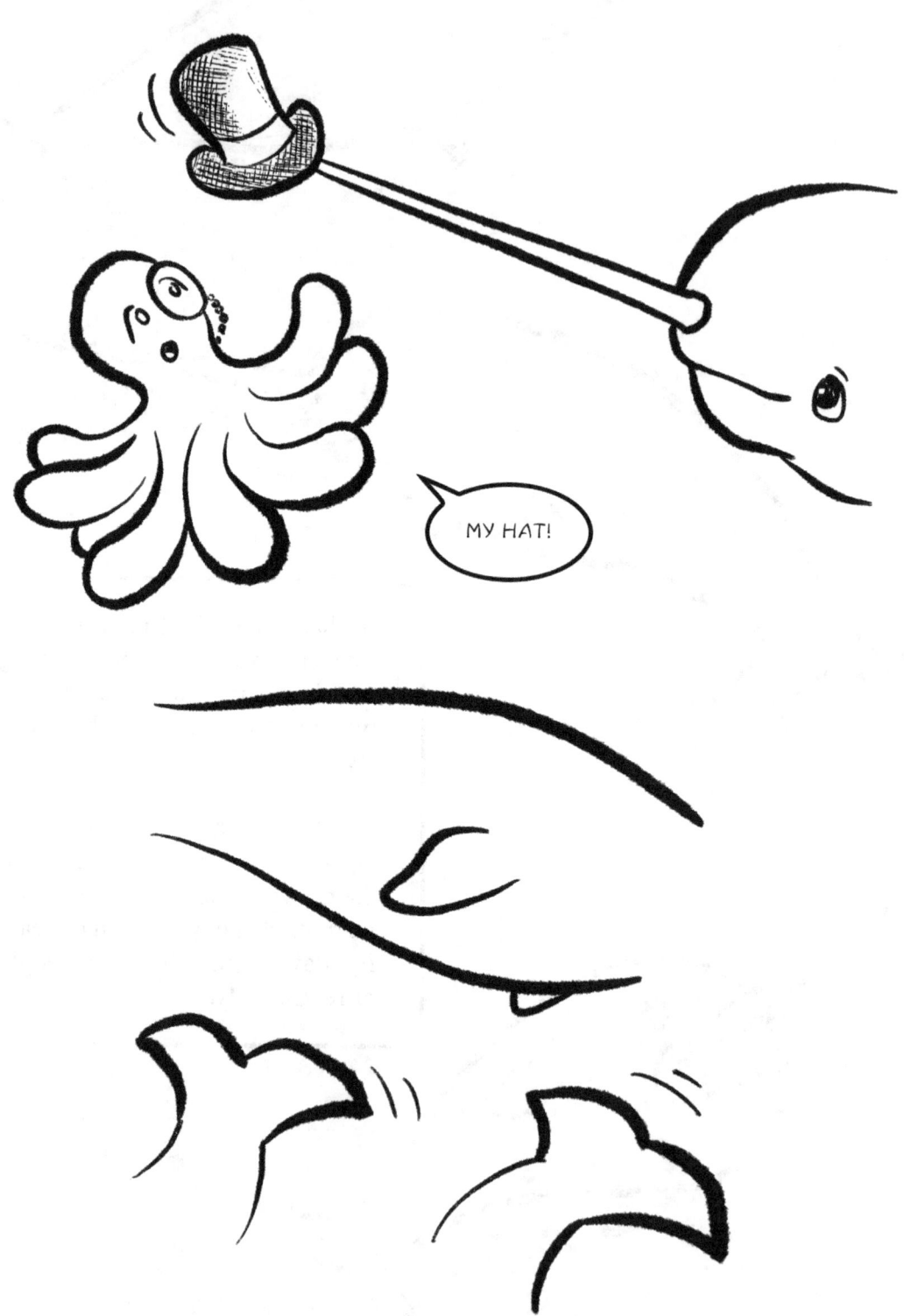

I'll cover proportions in the next section, but I like to break my narwhal drawings into three parts. How you draw these parts, and in what order, is entirely up to you, though I typically draw its head first, body, and then the tail.

1. Head
2. Body
3. Tail

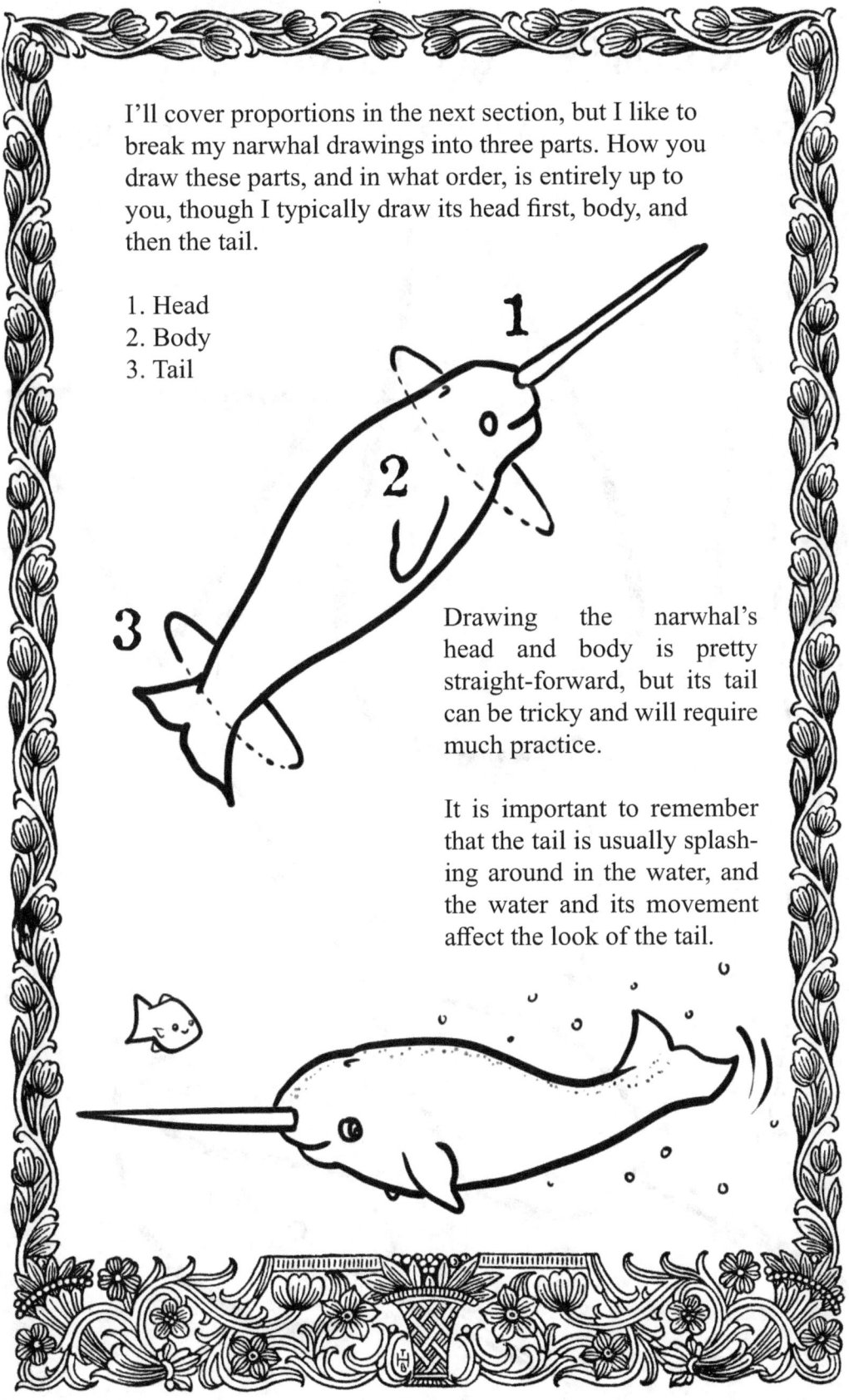

Drawing the narwhal's head and body is pretty straight-forward, but its tail can be tricky and will require much practice.

It is important to remember that the tail is usually splashing around in the water, and the water and its movement affect the look of the tail.

GEOMETRIC SHAPES

TOWER   TEARDROP   TRIANGLE

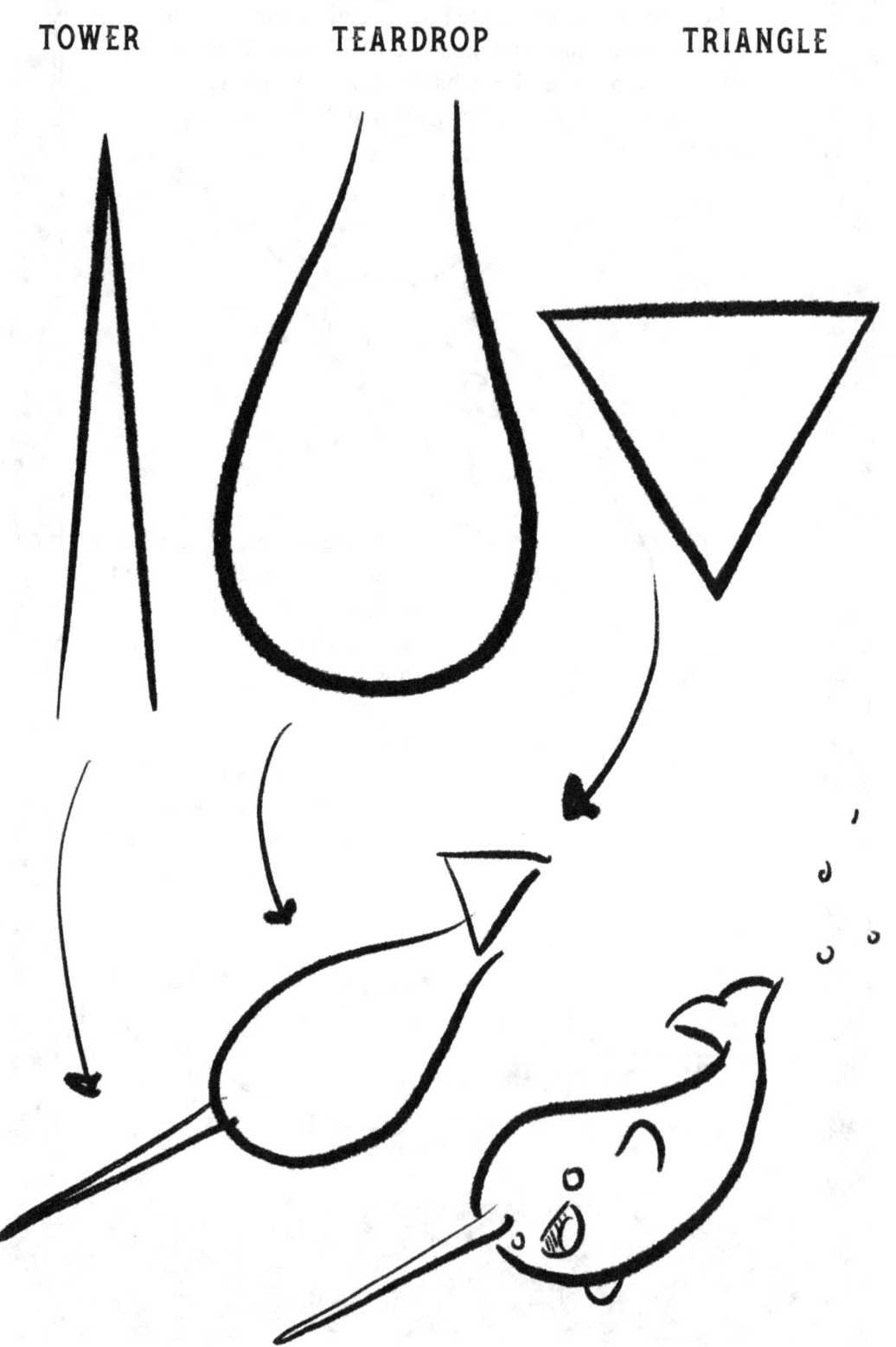

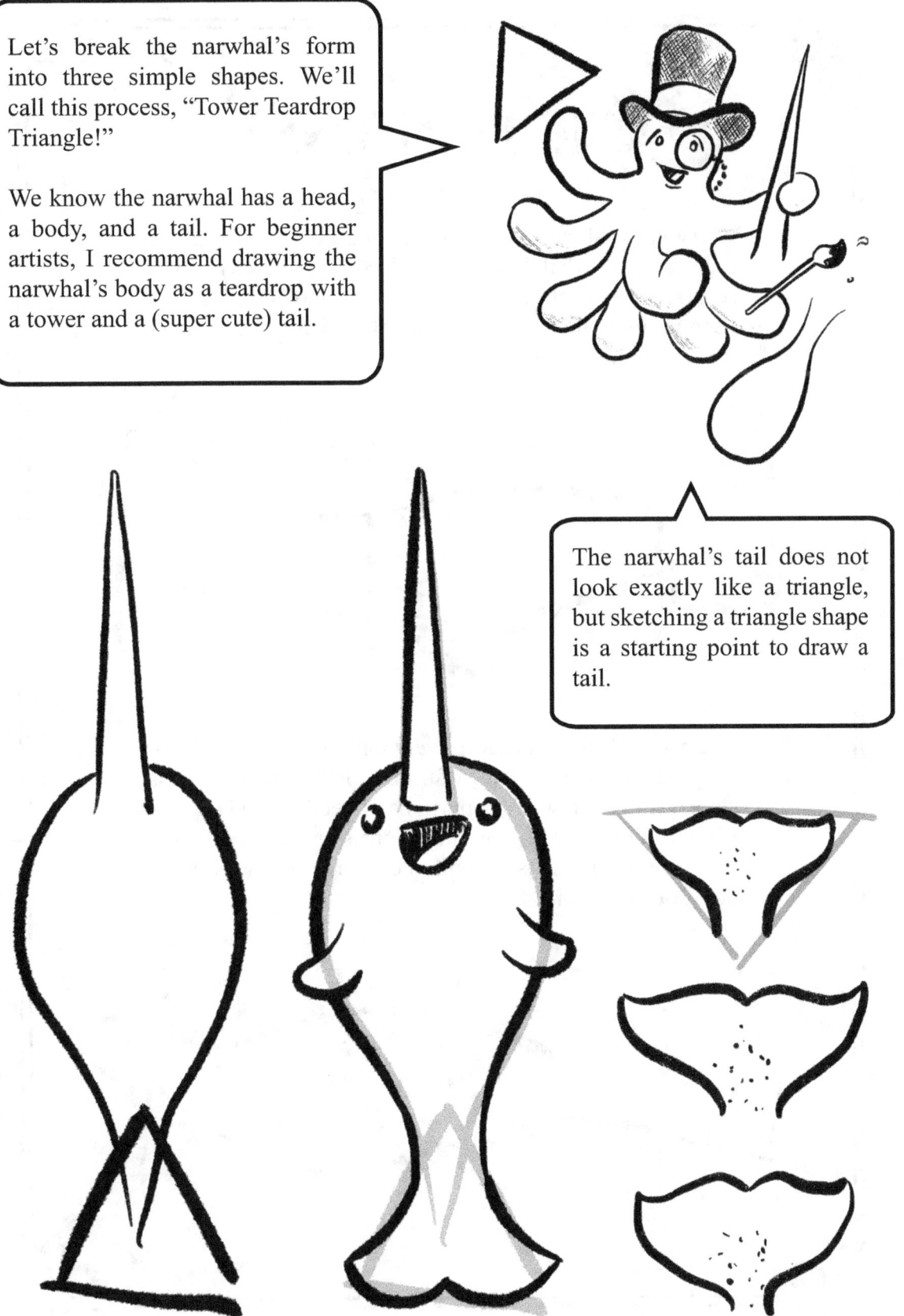

Proportions

Every narwhal is different, but a good rule of thumb is to break each narwhal drawing into thirds as pictured below. I separate my sketches into the tail, head, and horn. Though, keep in mind, this is a rough guideline that the artist does not need to follow exactly.

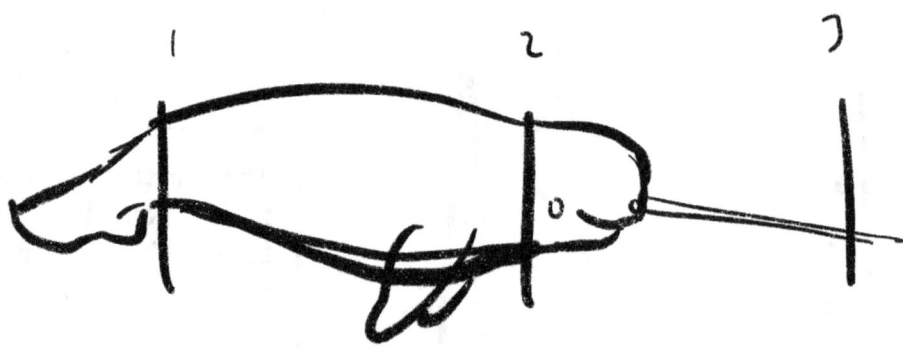

The narwhal's horn is deceptively long. Using a rough but simple guide like the "rule of thirds" demonstrated here is a good way to draw its proportions correctly. I find that my narwhal drawings are the most consistent when I follow the "rule of thirds," sketch the head first, followed by its body, tail, and horn.

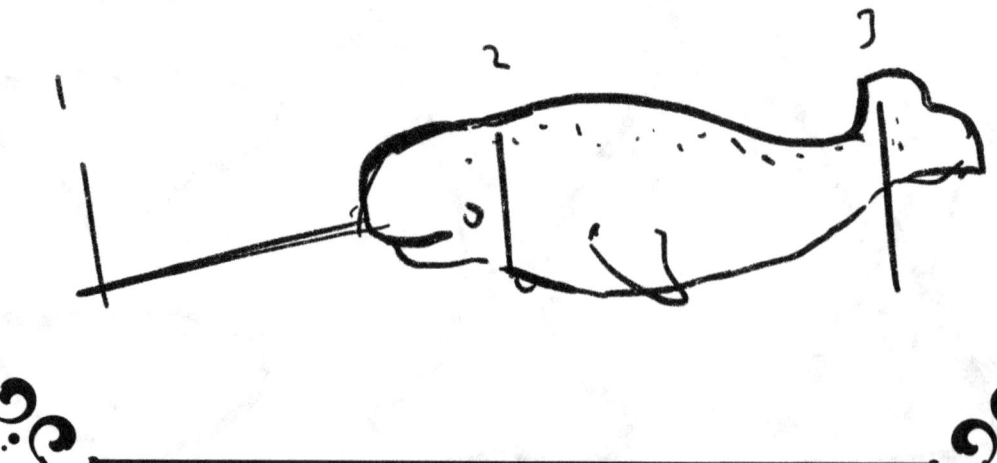

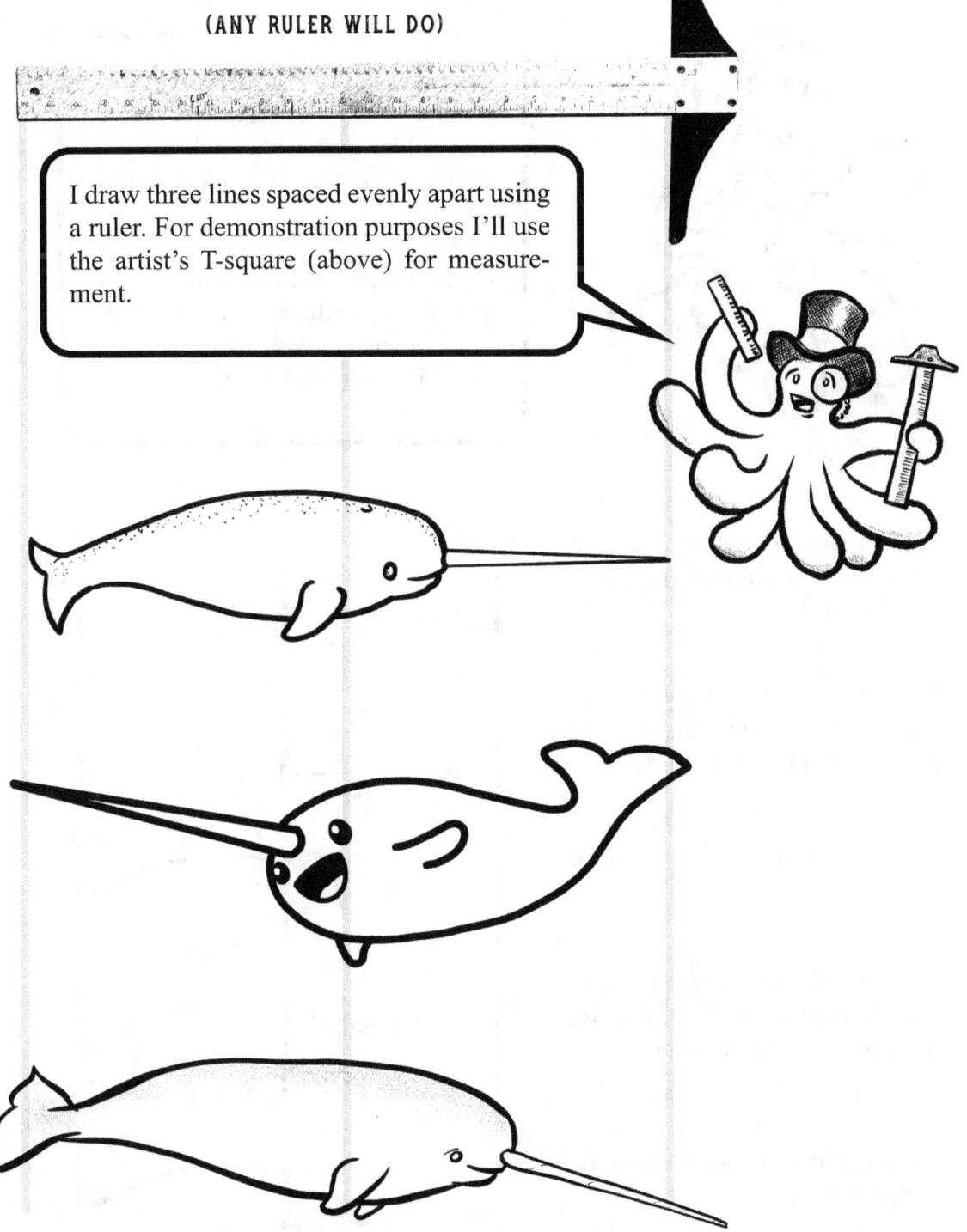

Step-By-Step

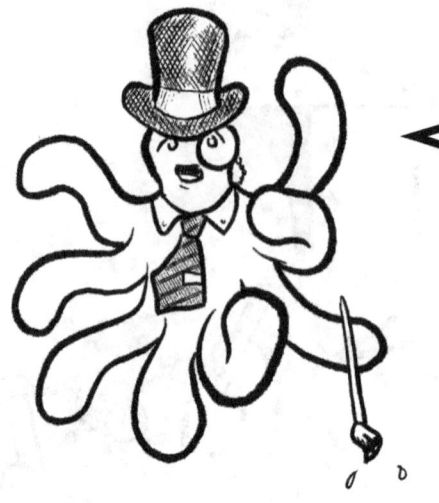

Now that we've learned about proportions and the basic geometric shapes that form a narwhal, lets put them all together in an easy-to-follow way.

I'll provide numerous examples for kawaii and realistic style narwhals to help inspire you on your narwhal-drawing adventure!

Let's draw three evenly spaced lines (as demonstrated in the previous section.)

I like to start by drawing the narwhal's head, which puts the rest of its body into perspective.

Next, I draw its teardrop-shaped body.

With my narwhal's head and body completed, I draw the tail using my guidelines for reference.

At last, I add the horn! There be narwhals here!

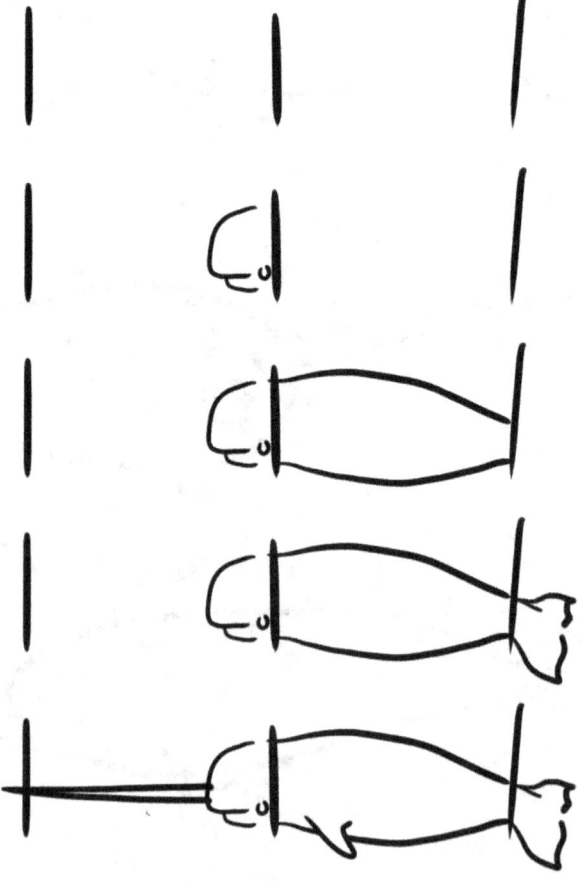

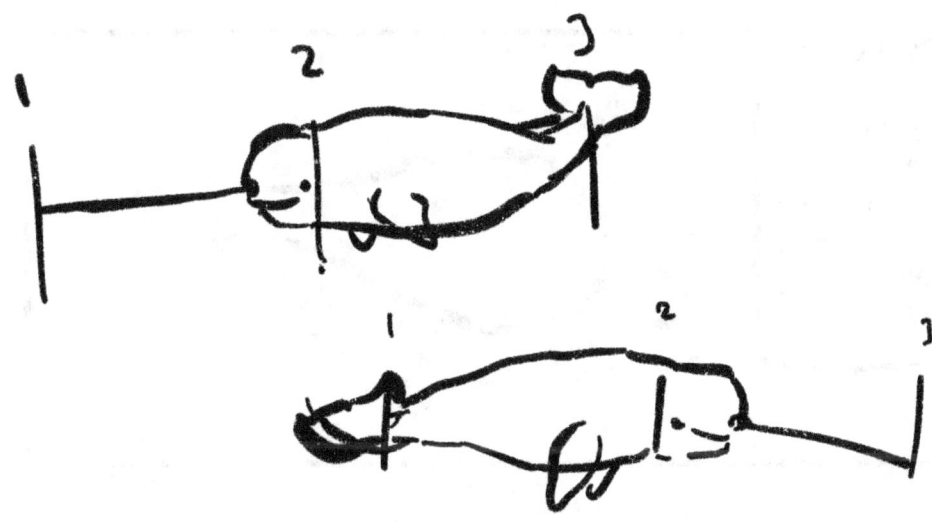

These three guidelines are very helpful when starting your narwhal drawing journey, however you may not want to see them in the finished drawing as seen below. Where did the guidelines go? I erased them!

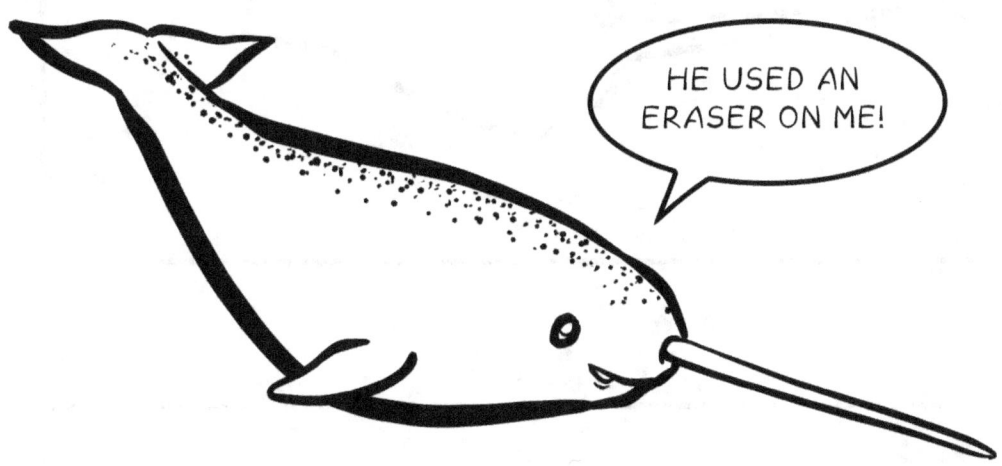

HE USED AN ERASER ON ME!

Consider sketching your three guidelines in pencil before drawing your completed narwhal (if you're drawing in pencil and ink.) Use light pencil strokes that are easy to erase when you're done with them.

You can even sketch out your entire design (or sketch) in pencil and then ink over it and later, then erase the pencil. If you're drawing digitally, you can work in multiple layers and "hide" your sketch layer. Practice and see what works for you!

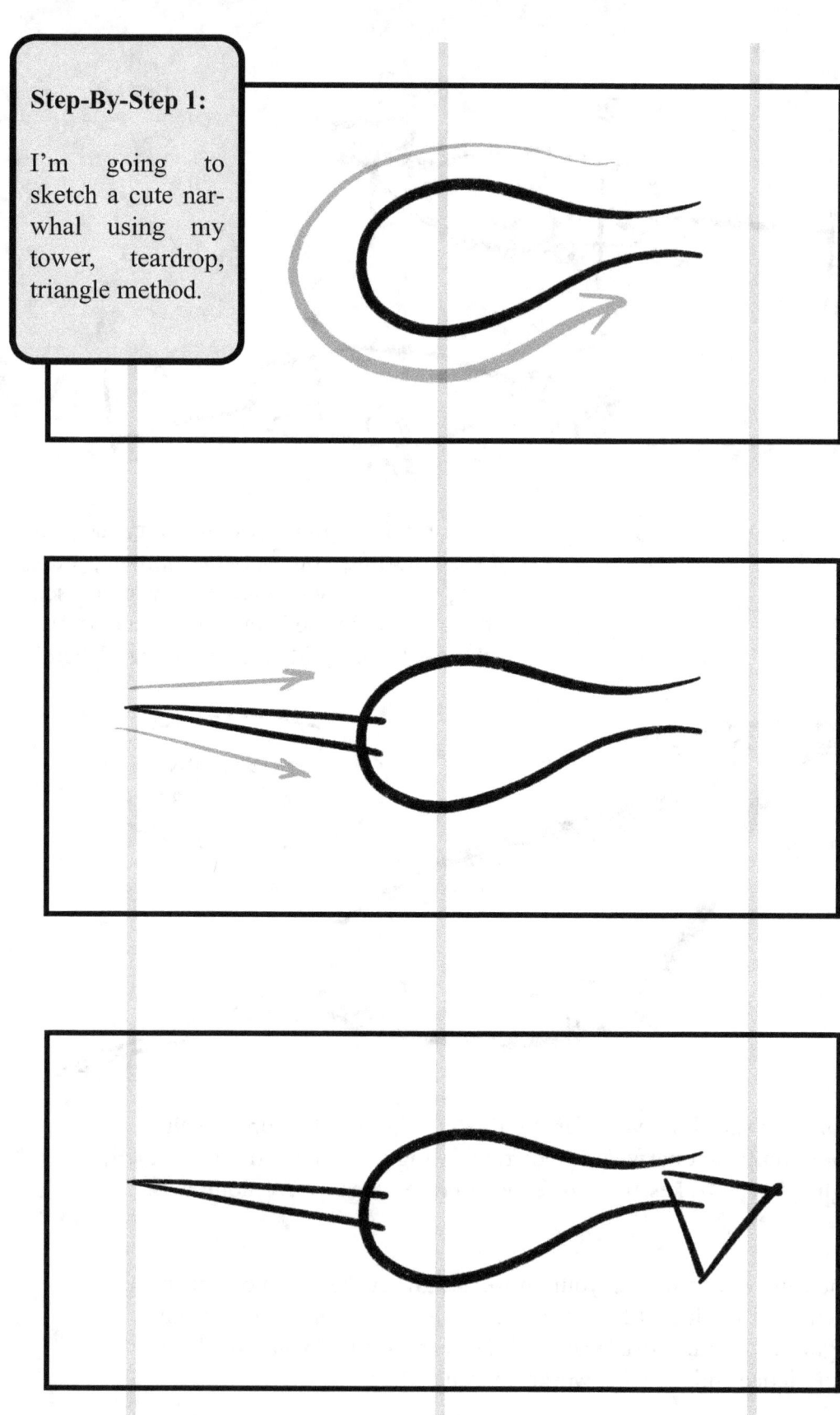

Step-By-Step 1:

I'm going to sketch a cute narwhal using my tower, teardrop, triangle method.

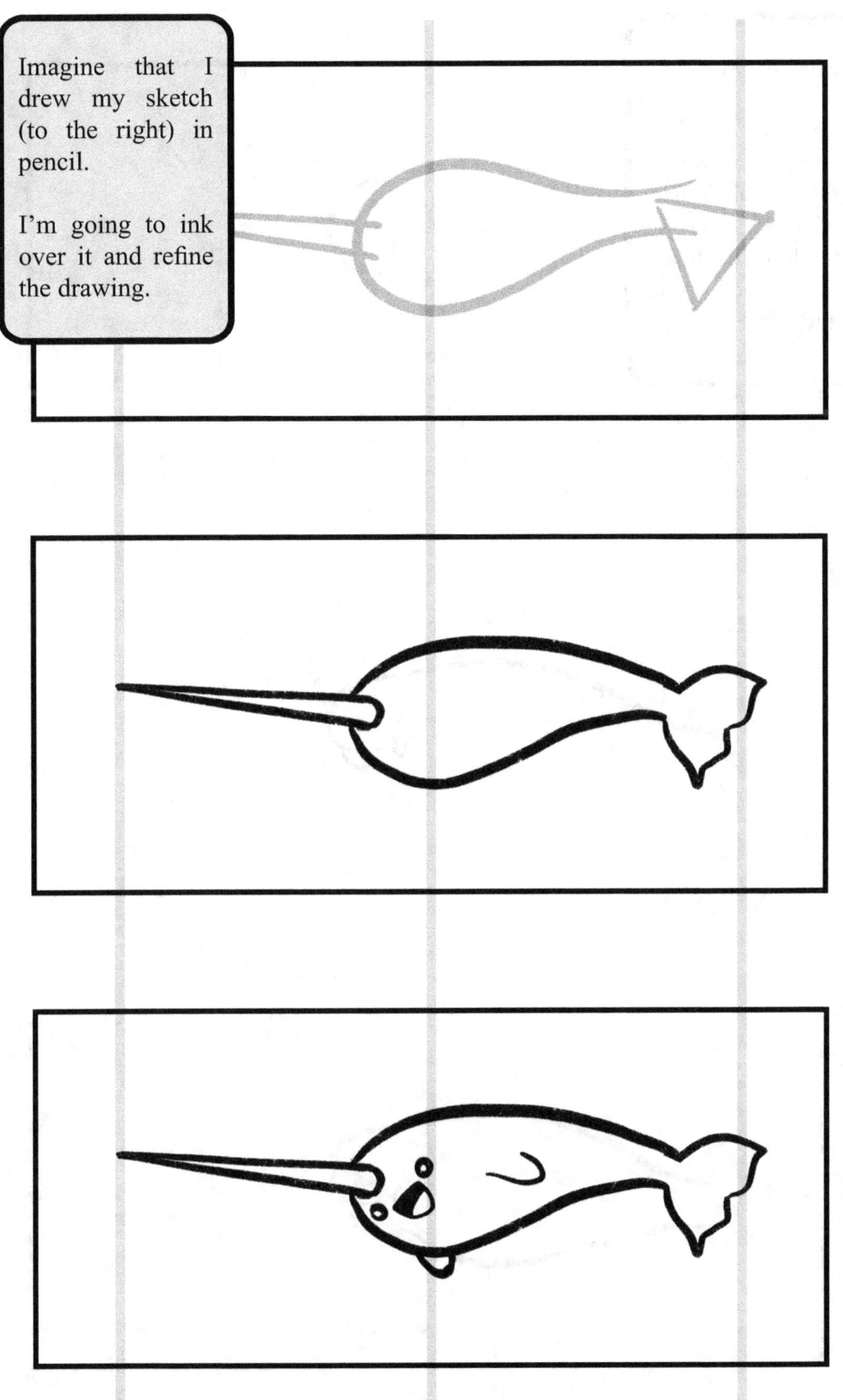

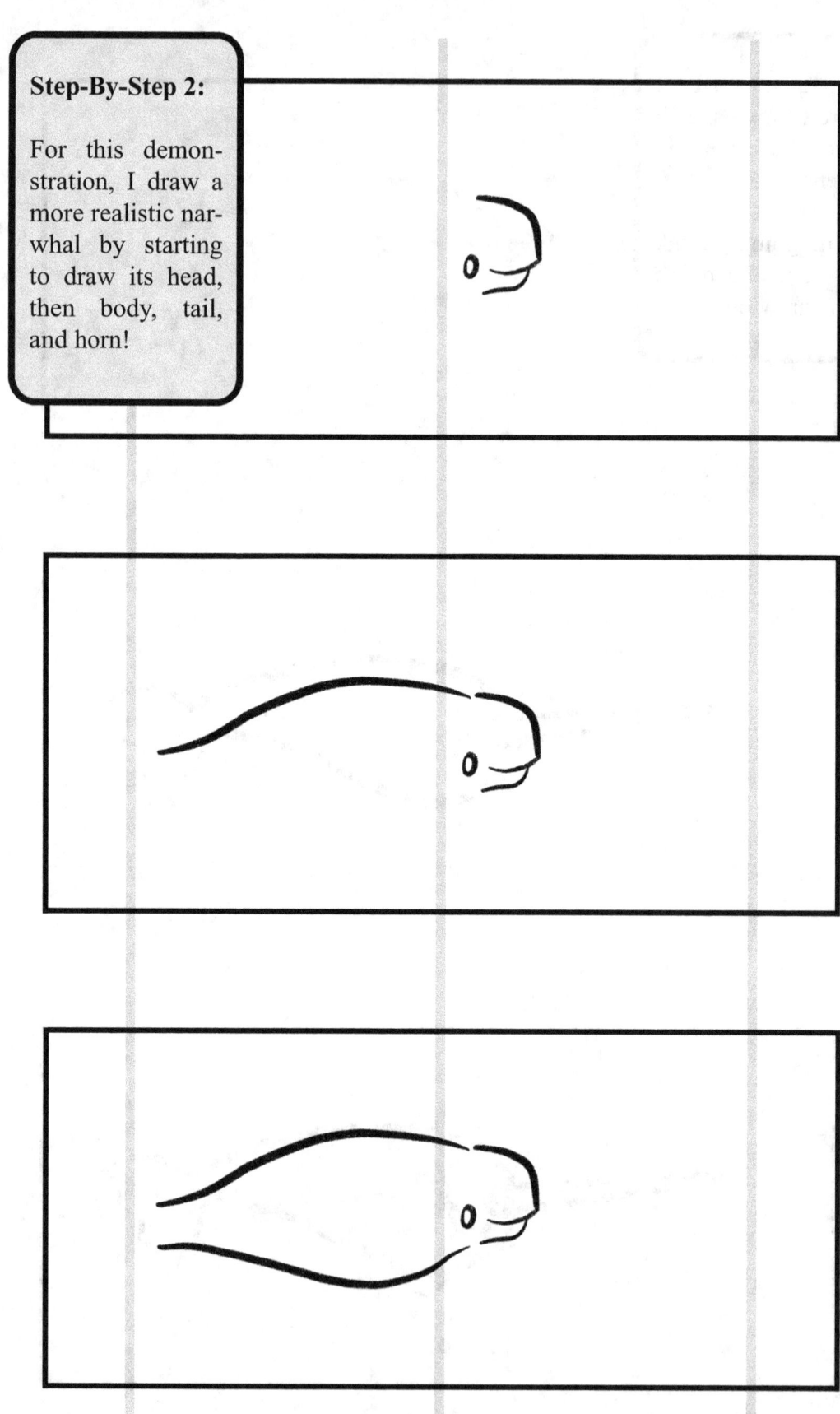

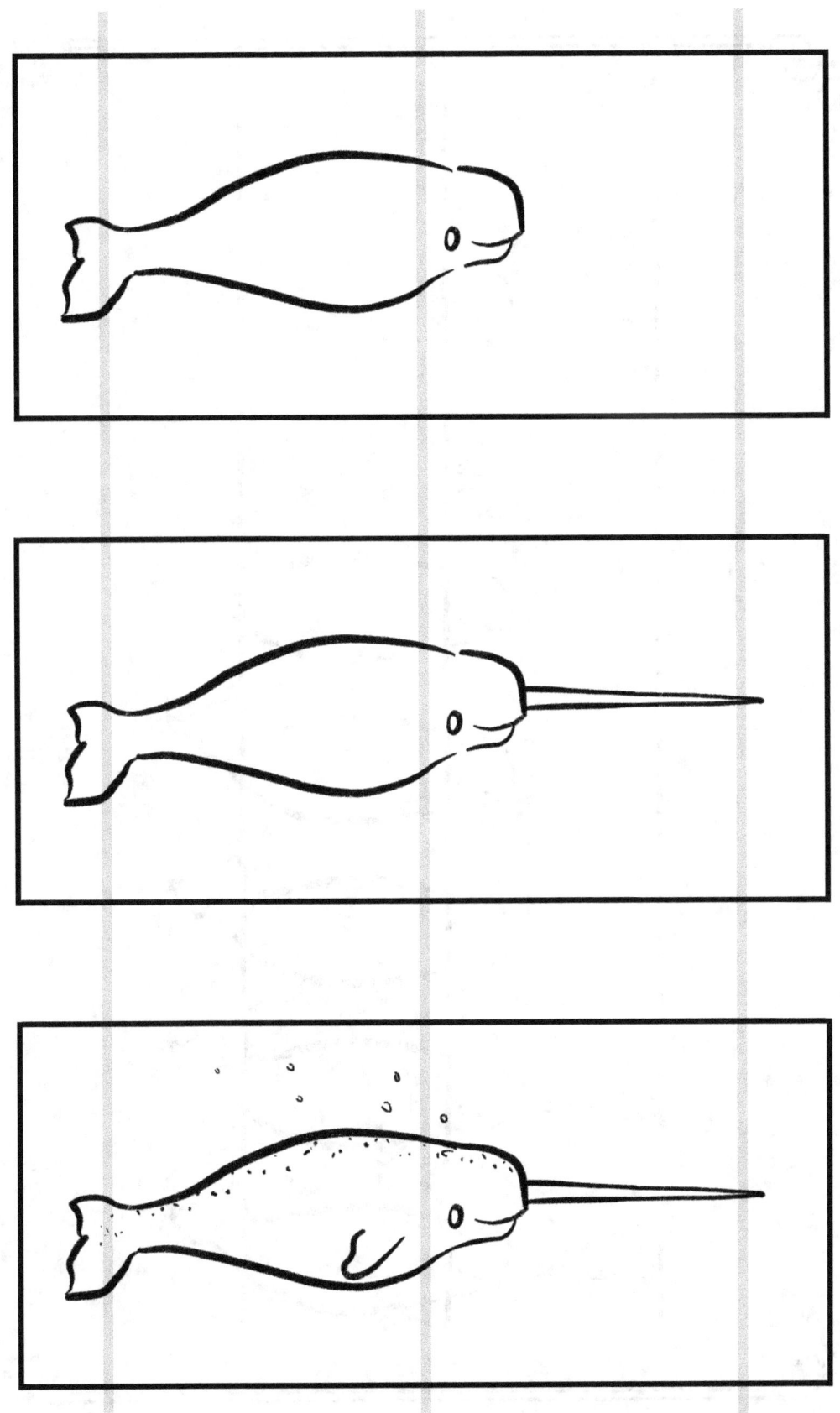

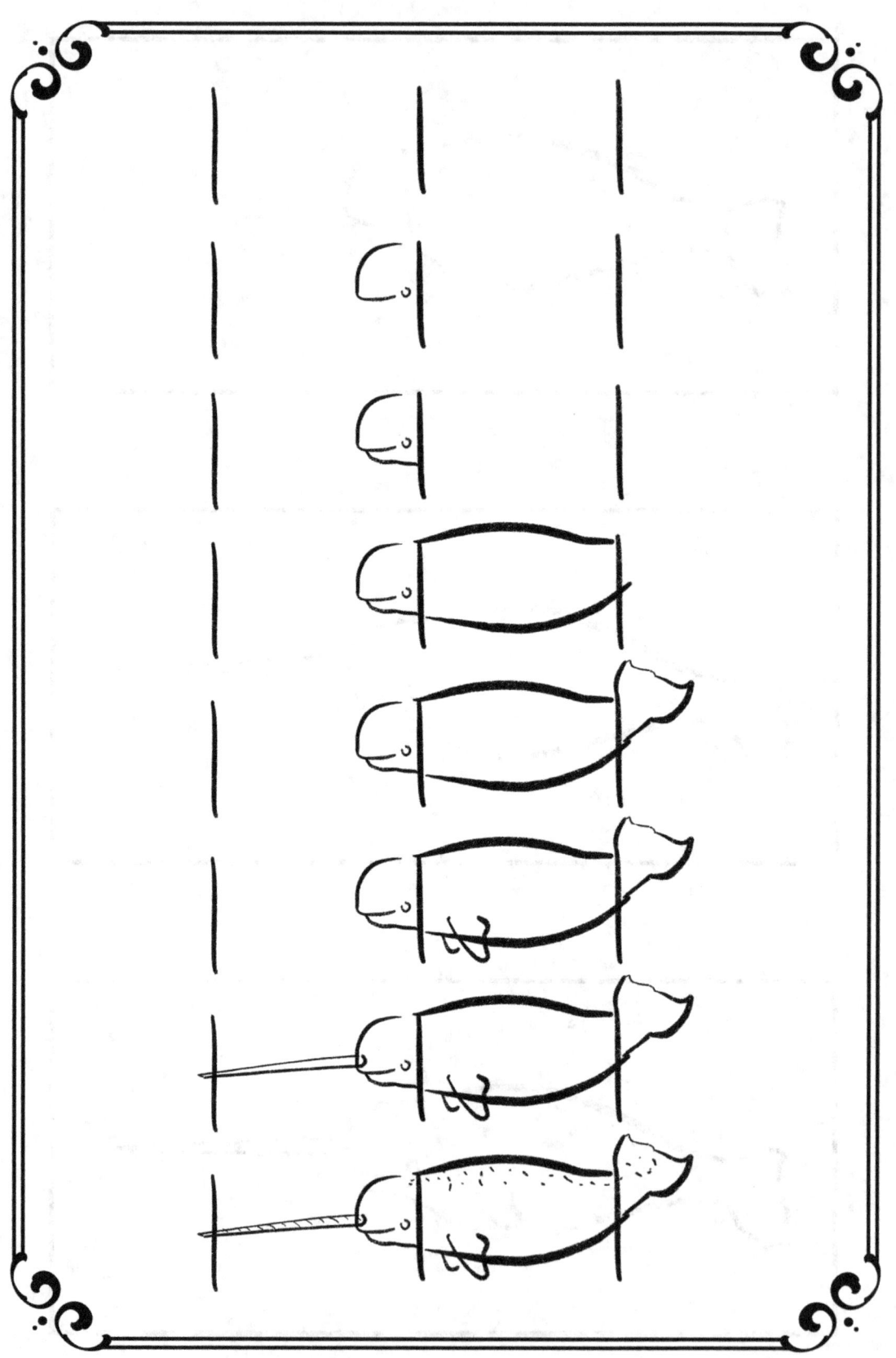

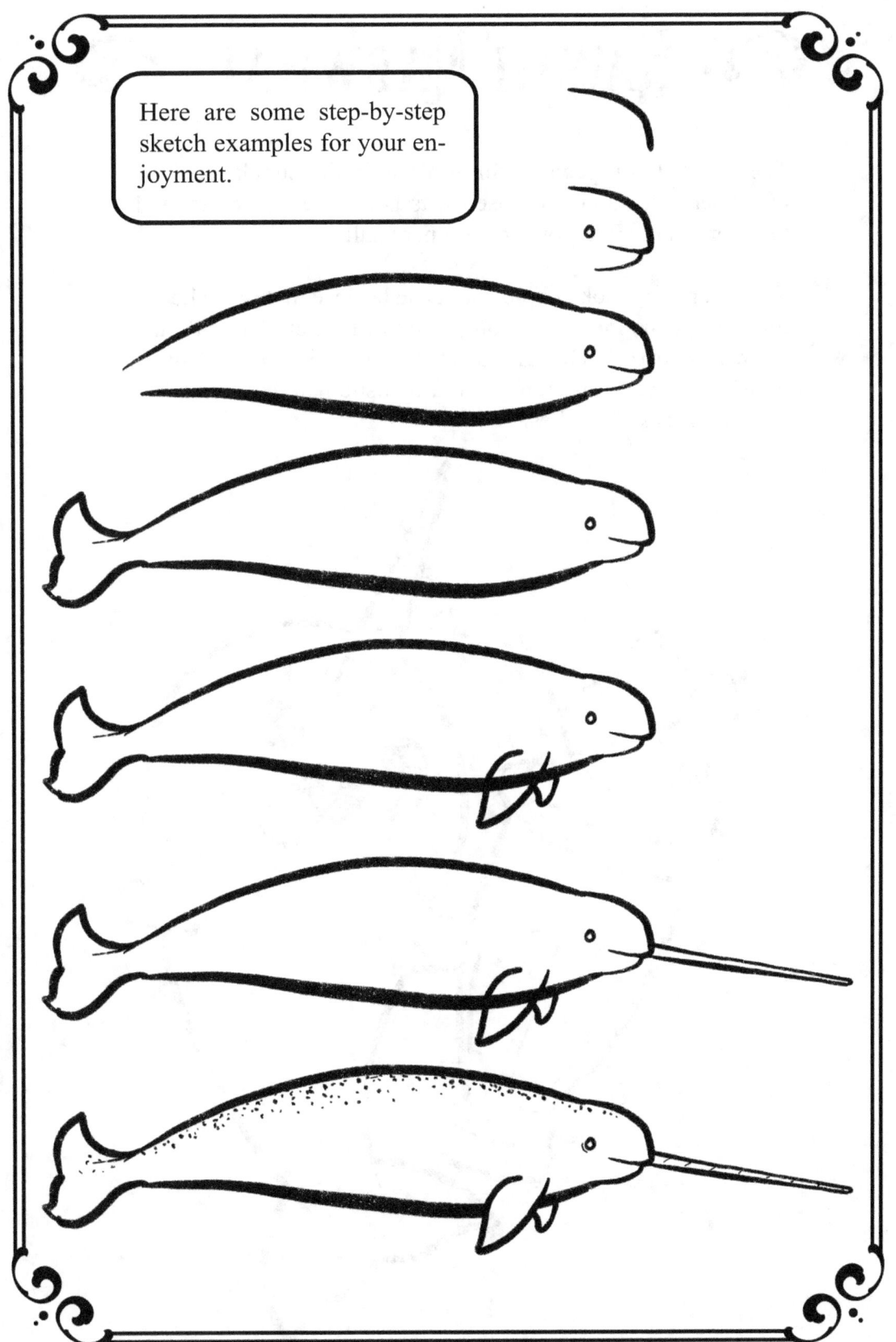

Kawaii Narwhal

The narwhal is especially fun to draw in the popular kawaii, or "super cute" style because of its horn, friendly smile, and teardrop shape. Everyone loves a narwhal!

Kawaii art may look simple, but it can be deceptively challenging to draw the lovable teardrop form of the narwhal with just a few pen strokes. Though the shape and design of the kawaii narwhal are very different from a realistic narwhal, the basic rule of thirds still applies.

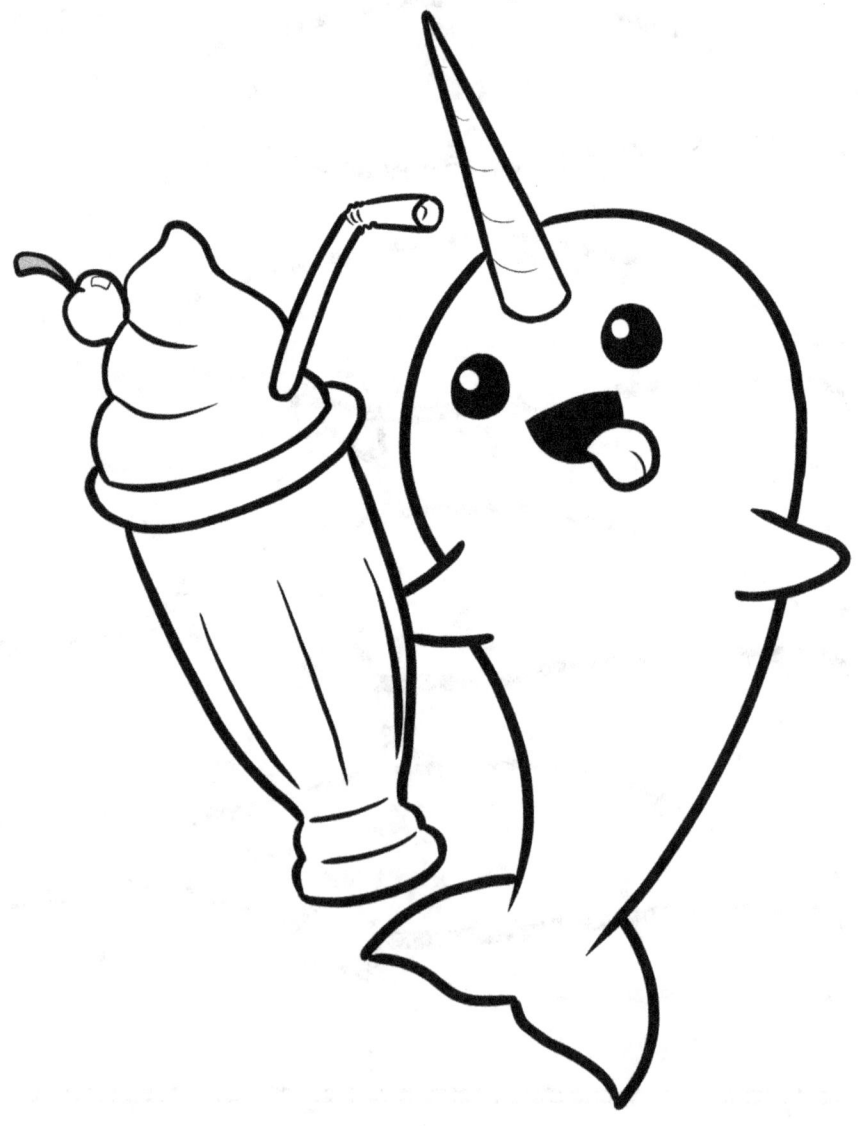

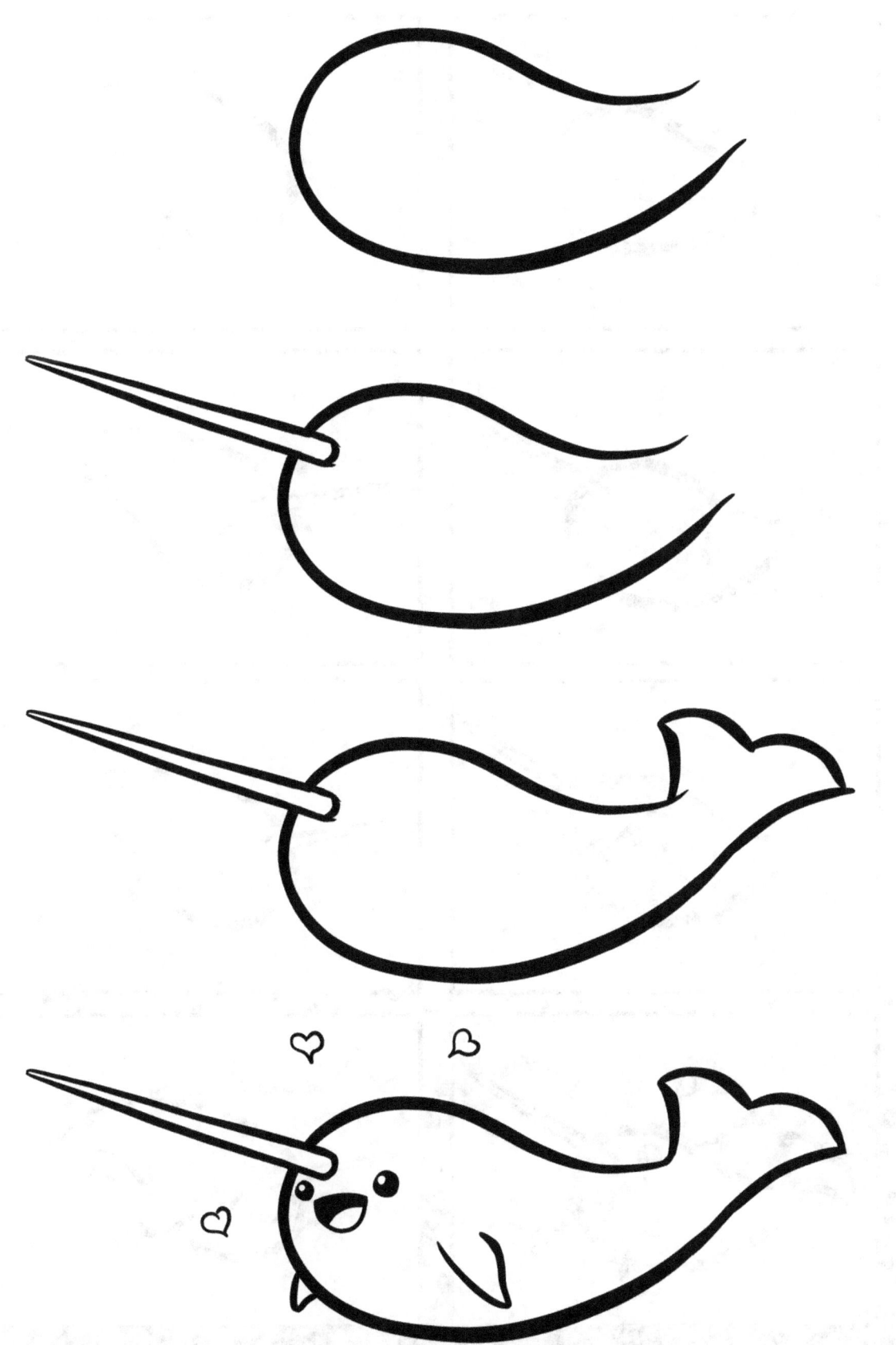

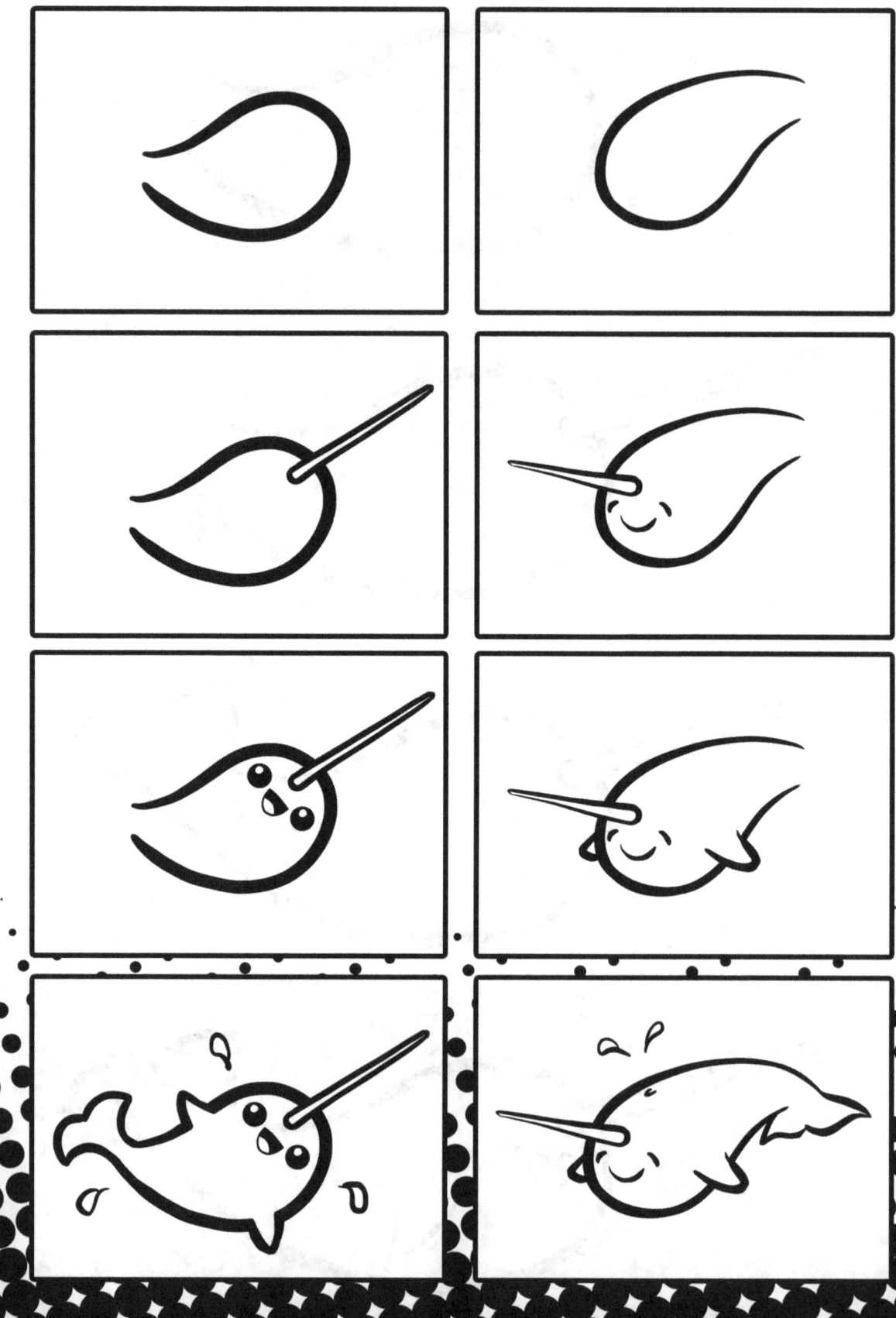

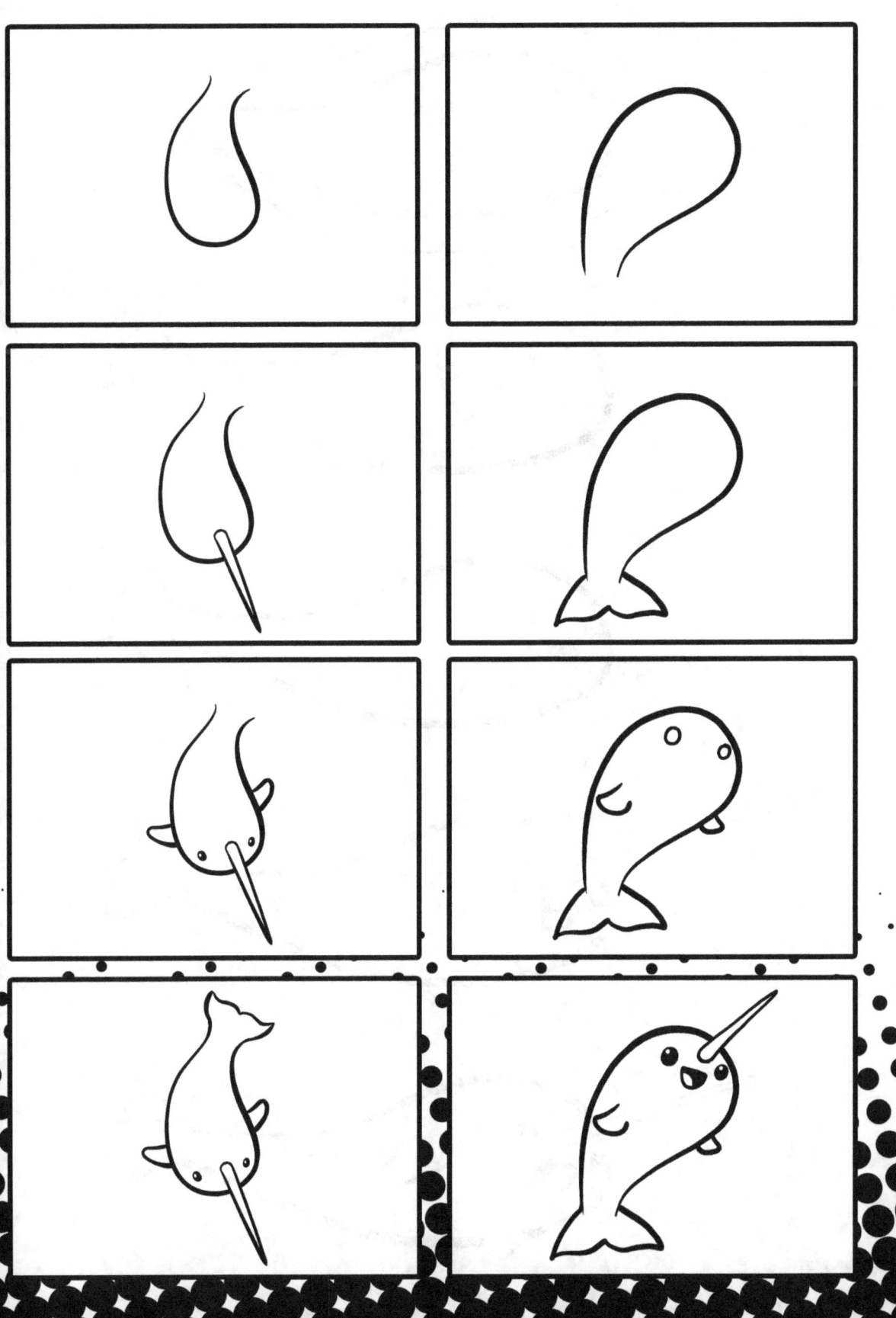

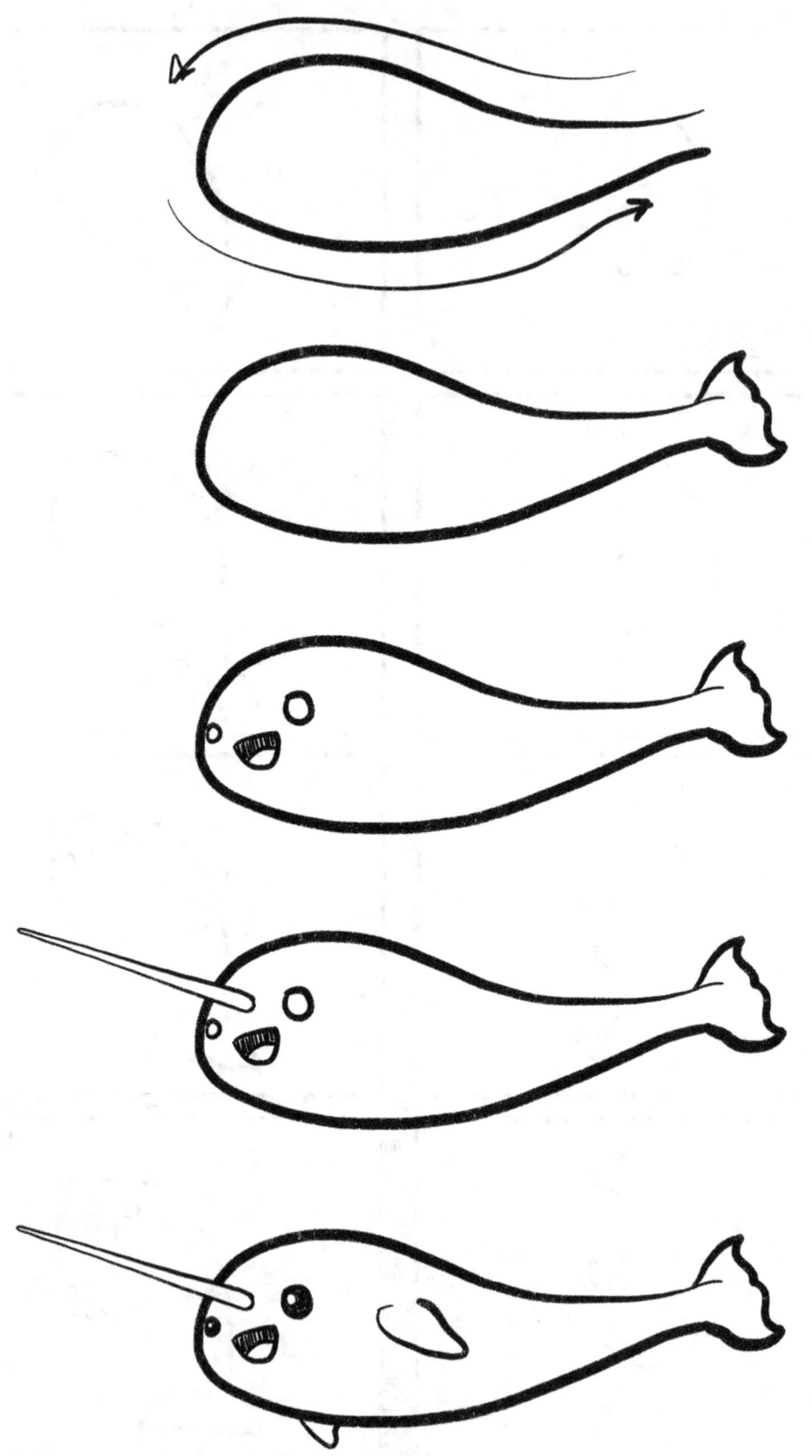

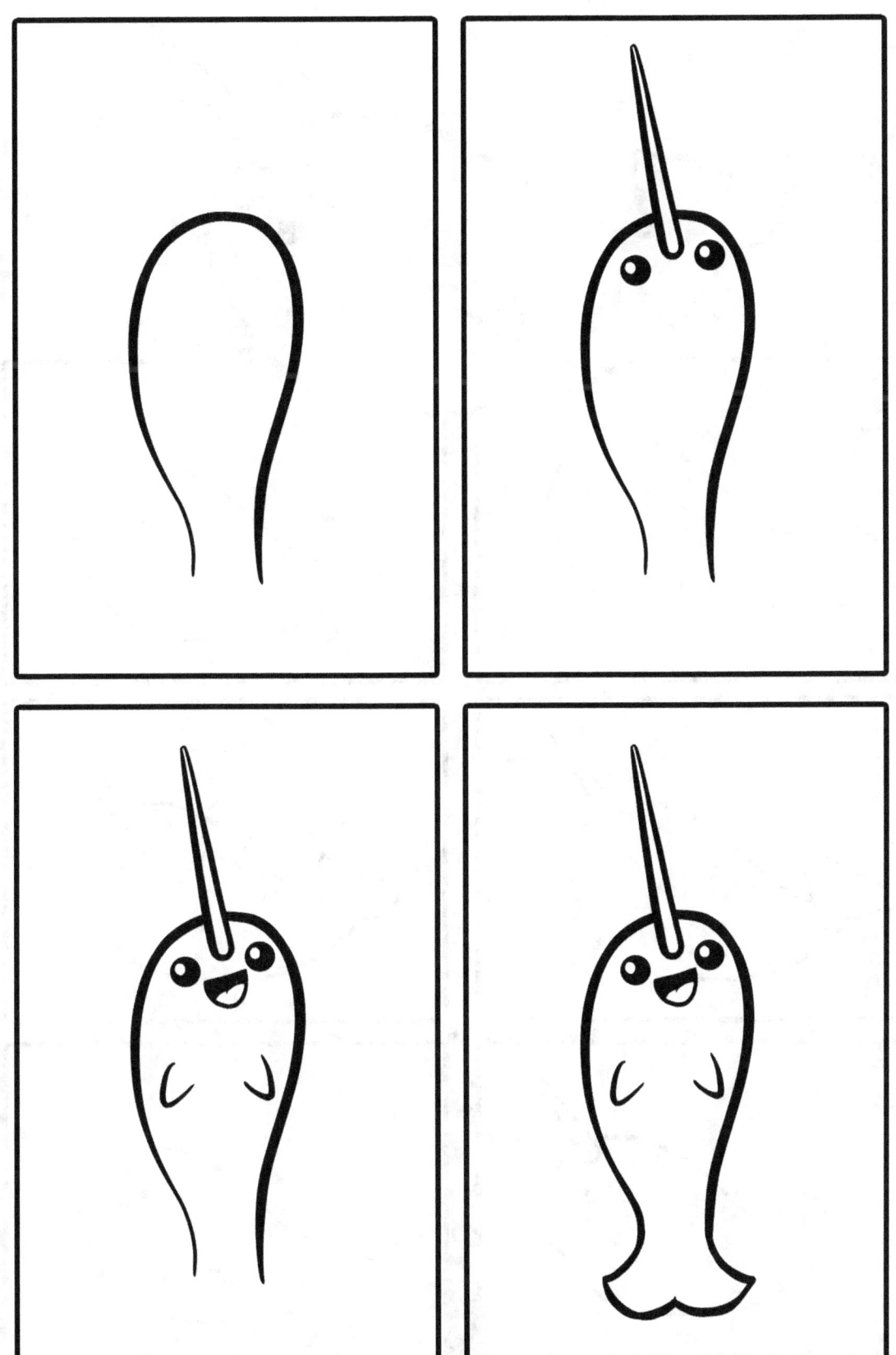

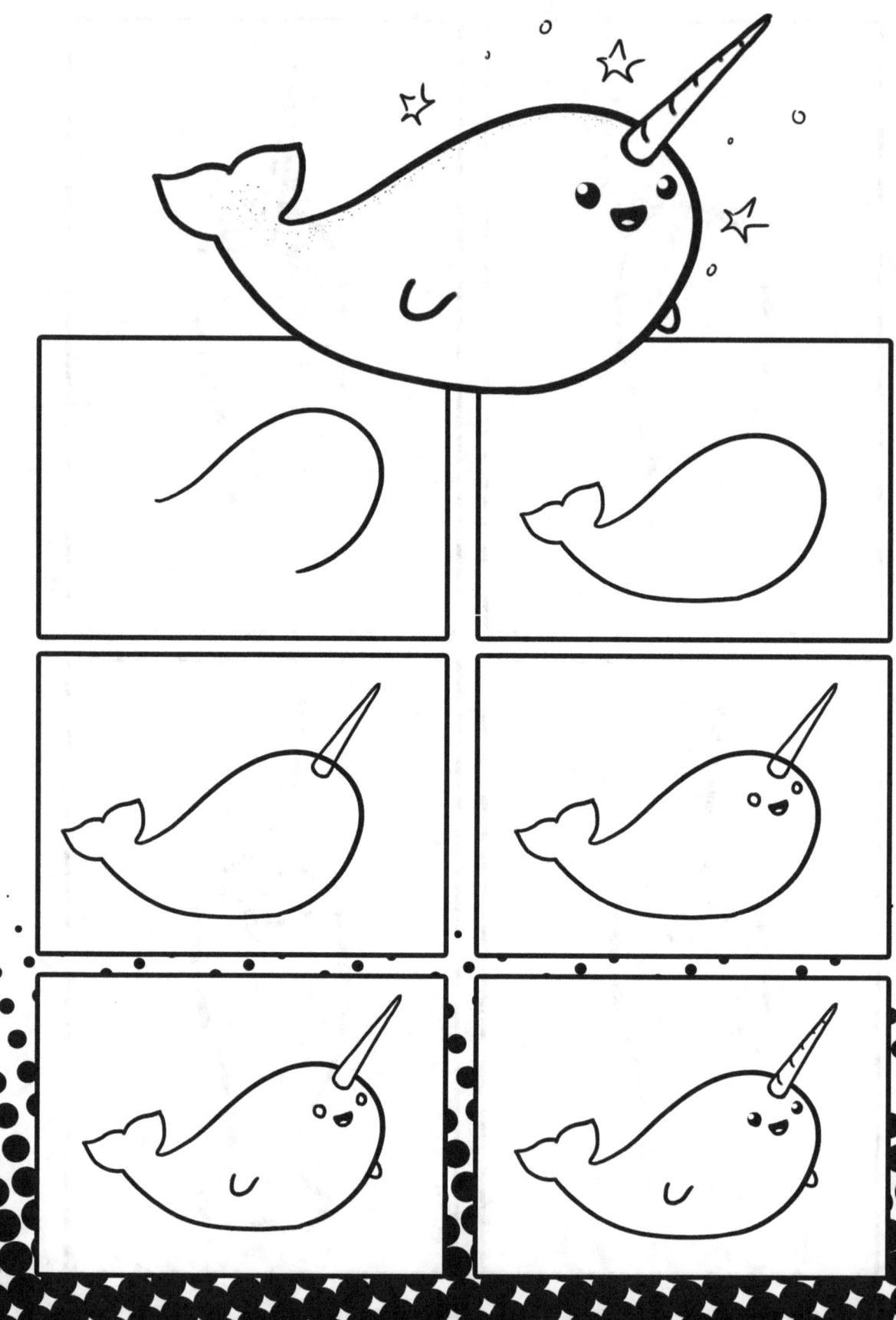

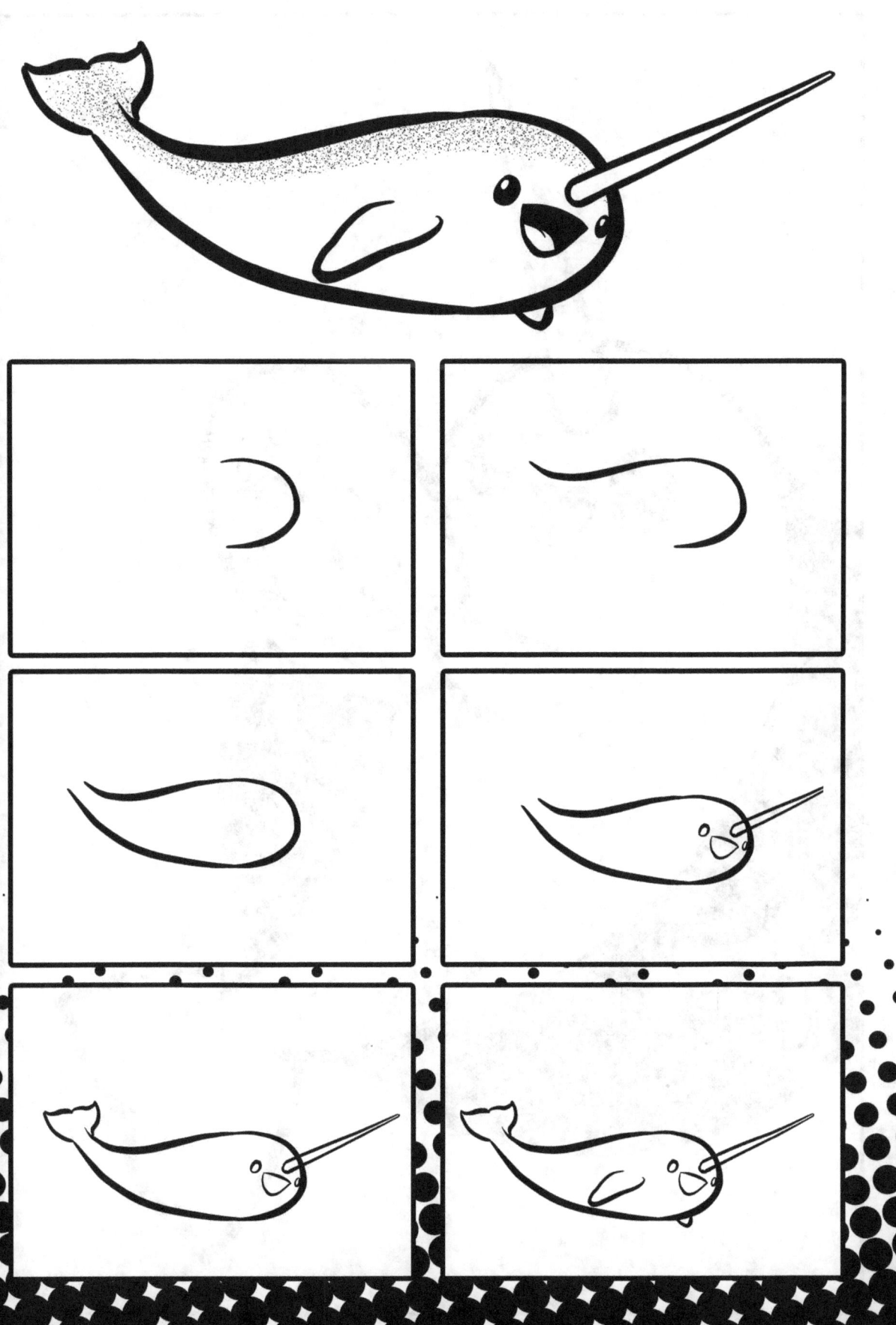

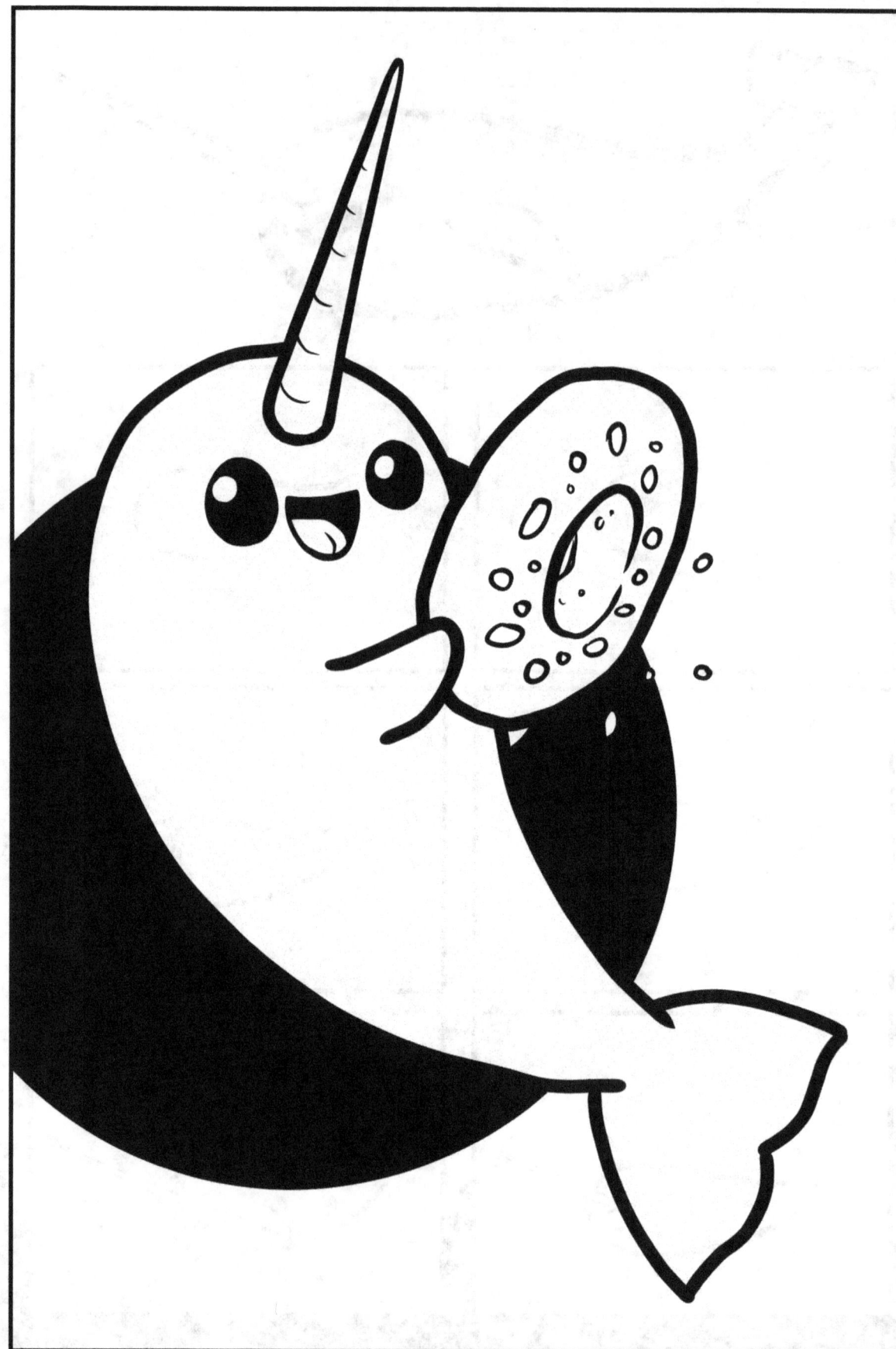

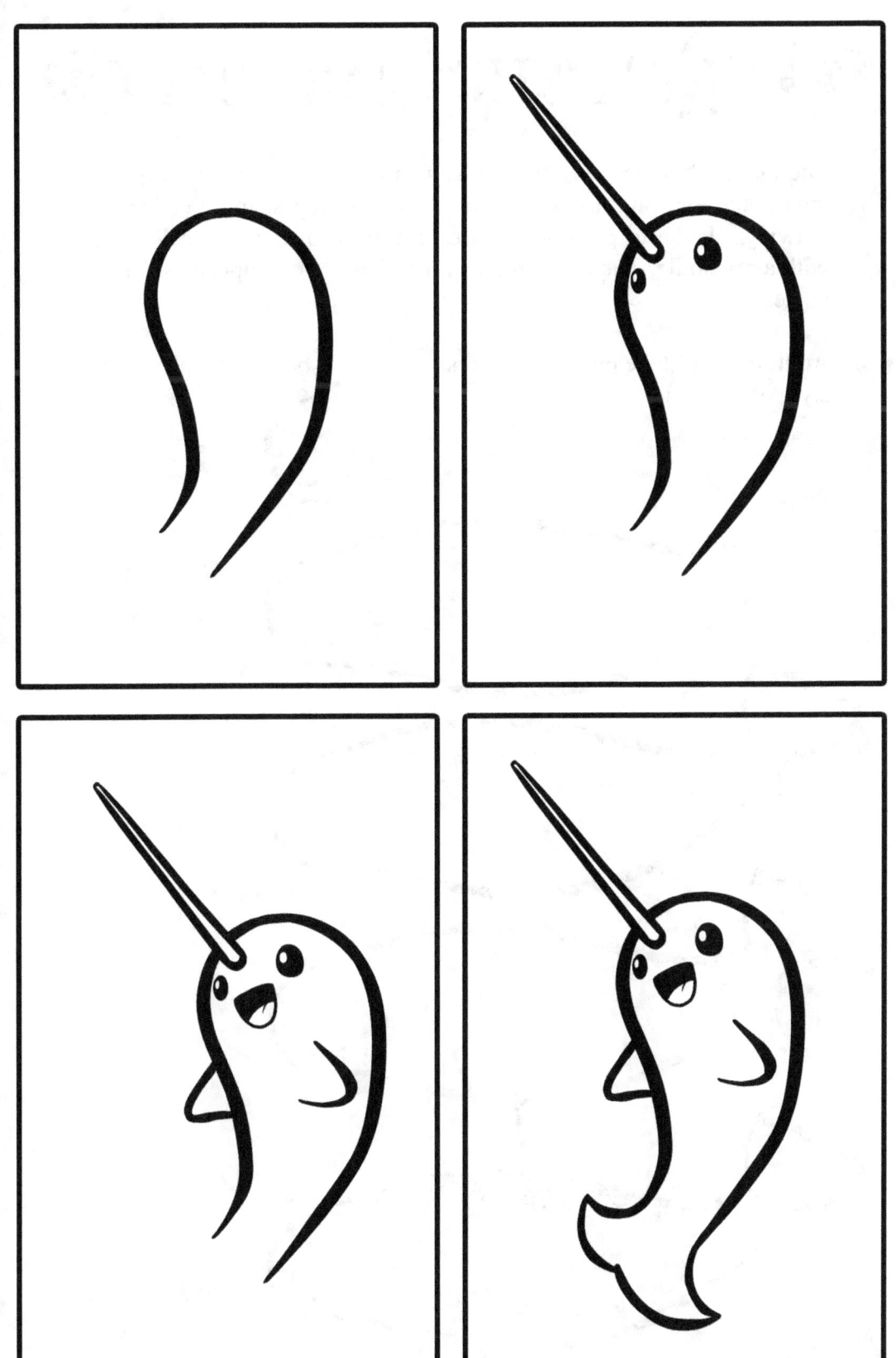

"Realistic" Narwhal

The main difference between my kawaii and realistic narwhal drawings is the eyes and exaggeration of the teardrop shape. For kawaii drawings, I like to put both eyes on the front of the narwhal's face with a big smile. The eyes on a real narwhal are on opposite sides of its head.

Additionally, I take more care to draw a realistic body and tail for this style of drawing.

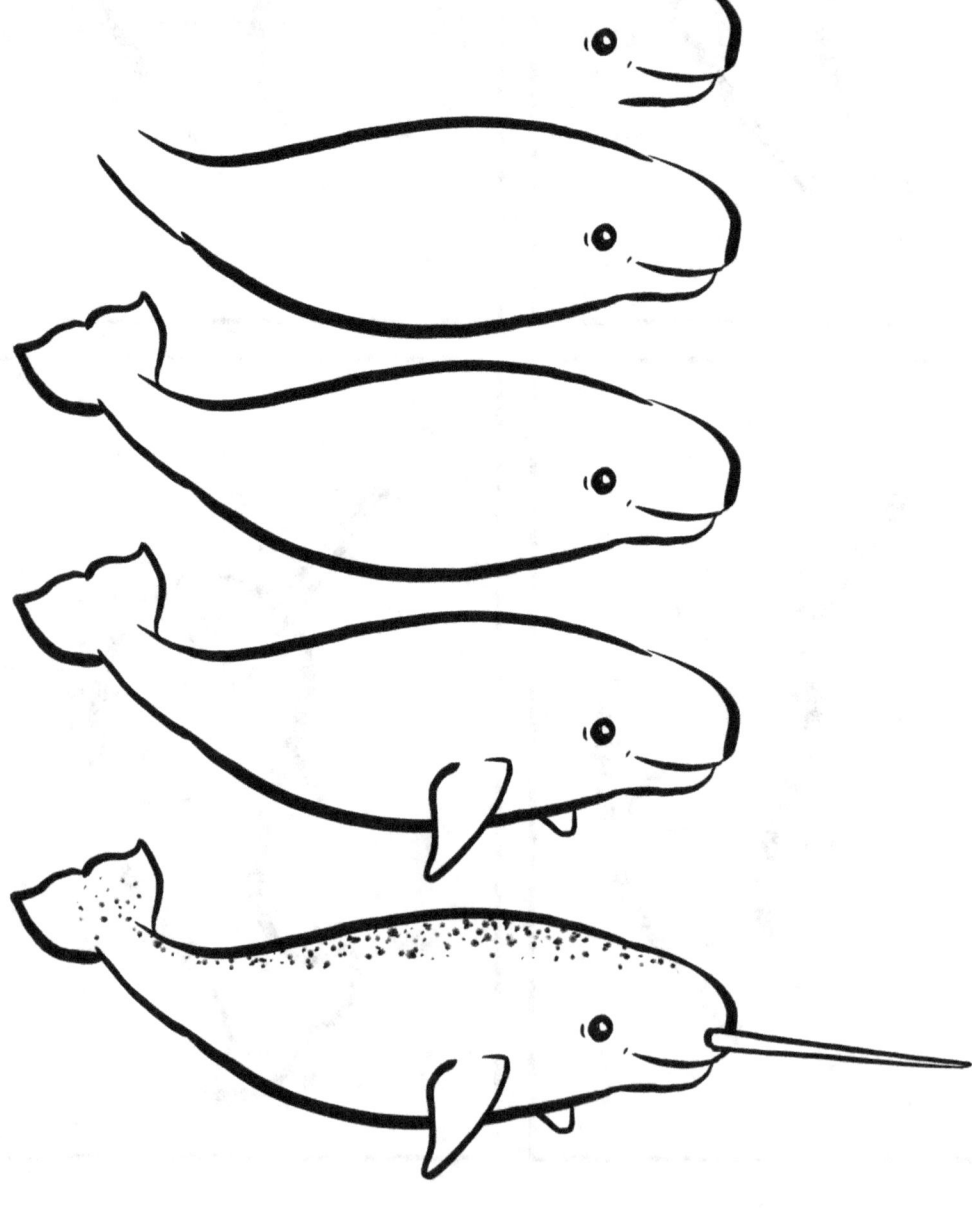

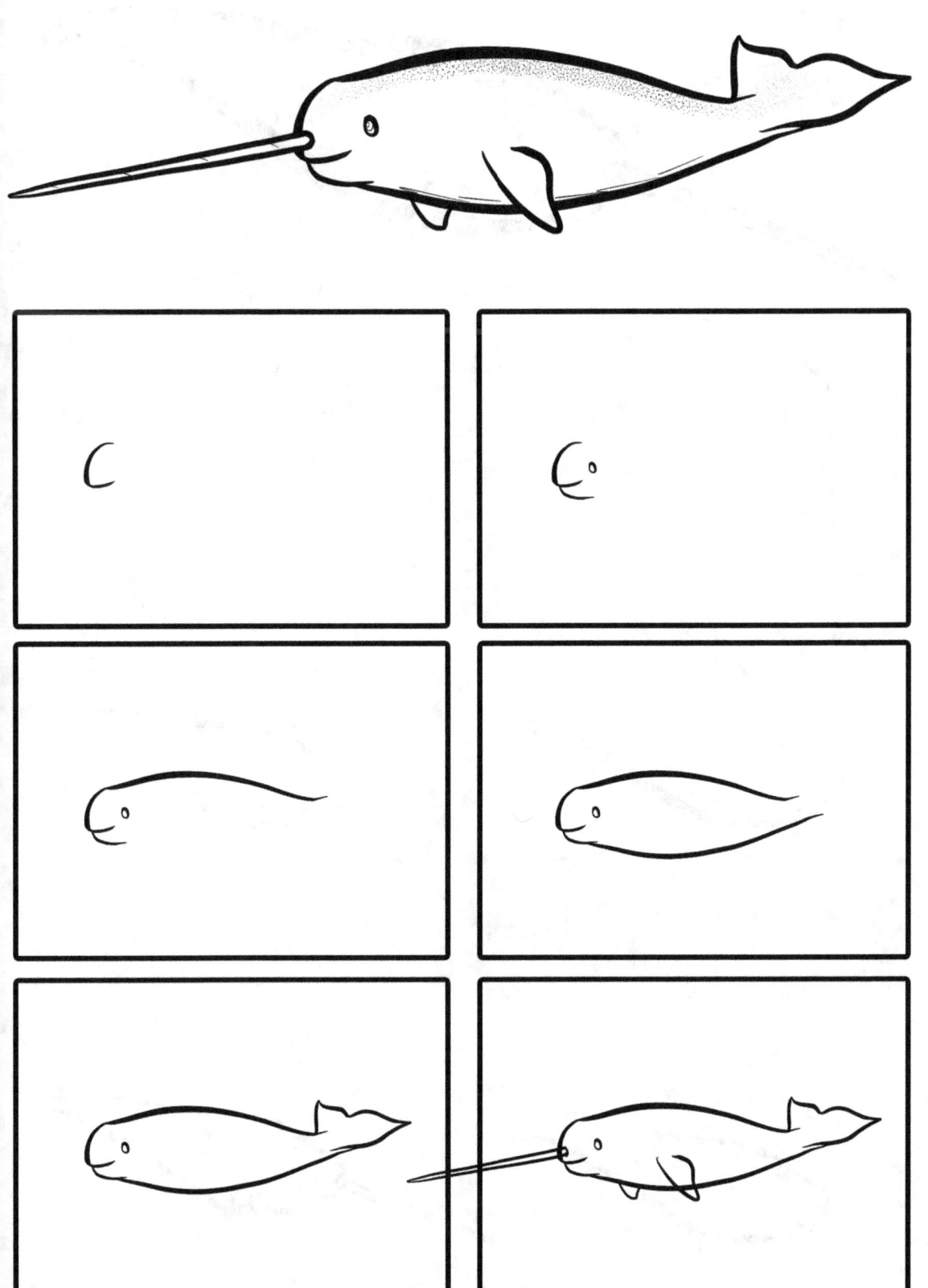

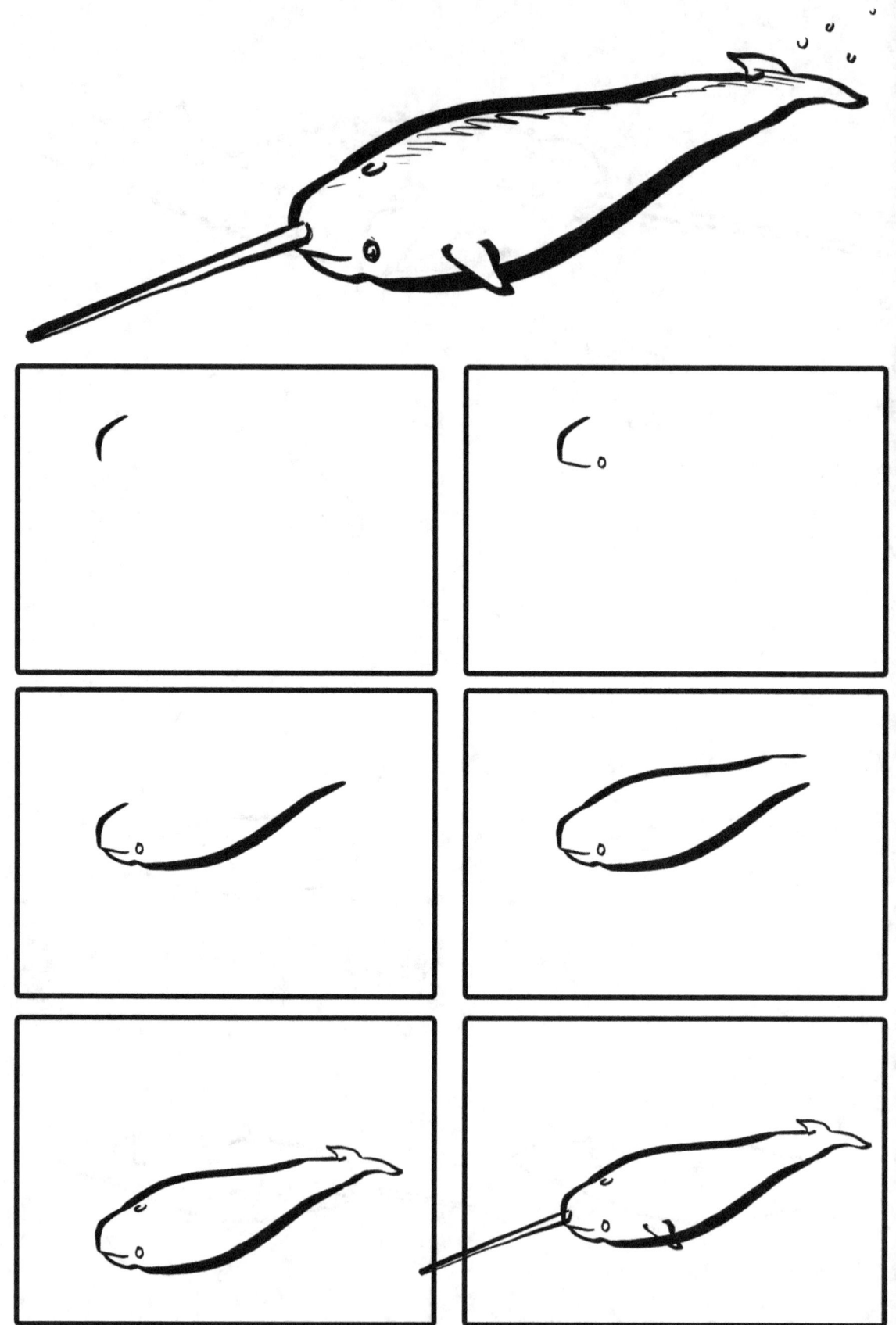

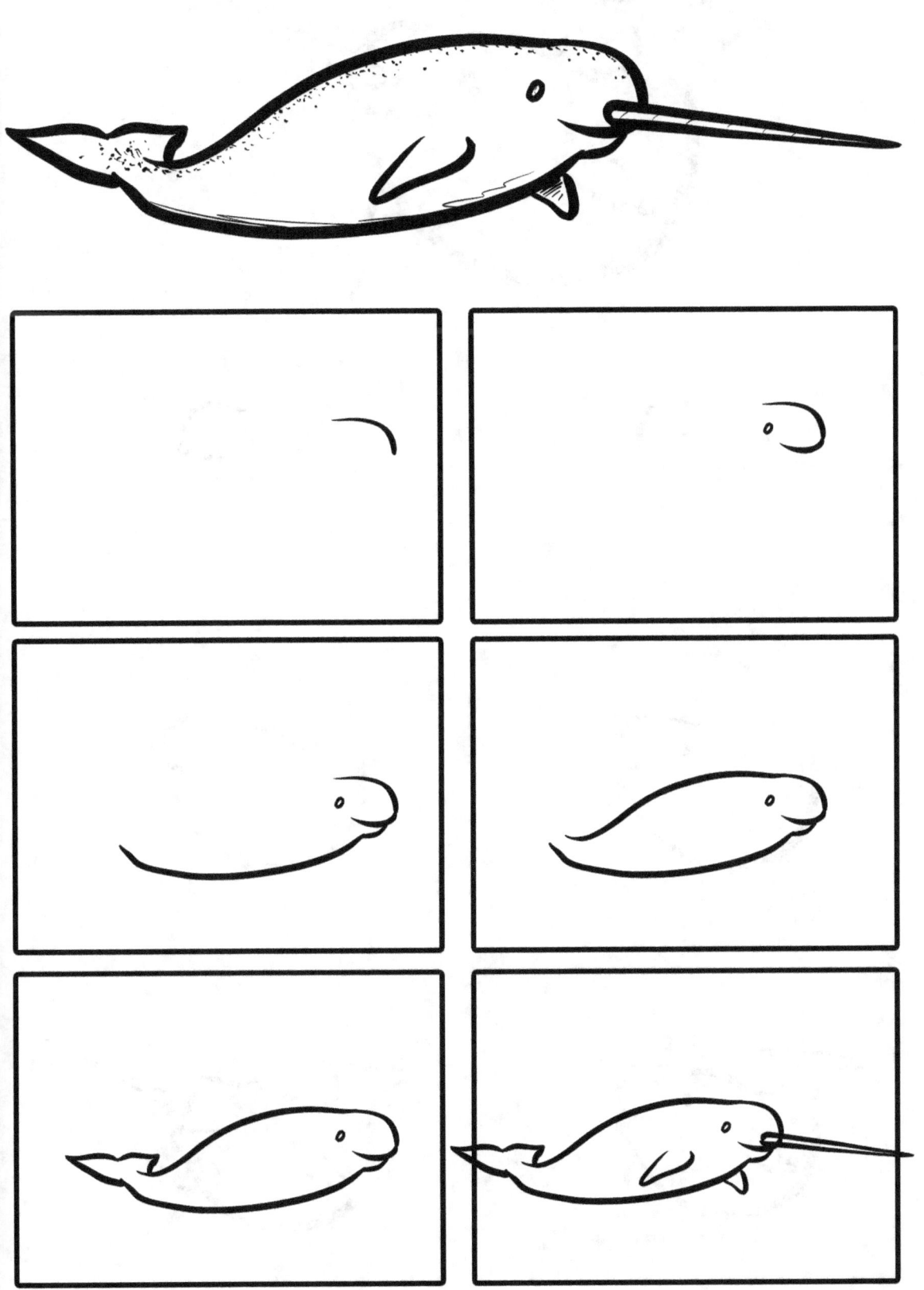

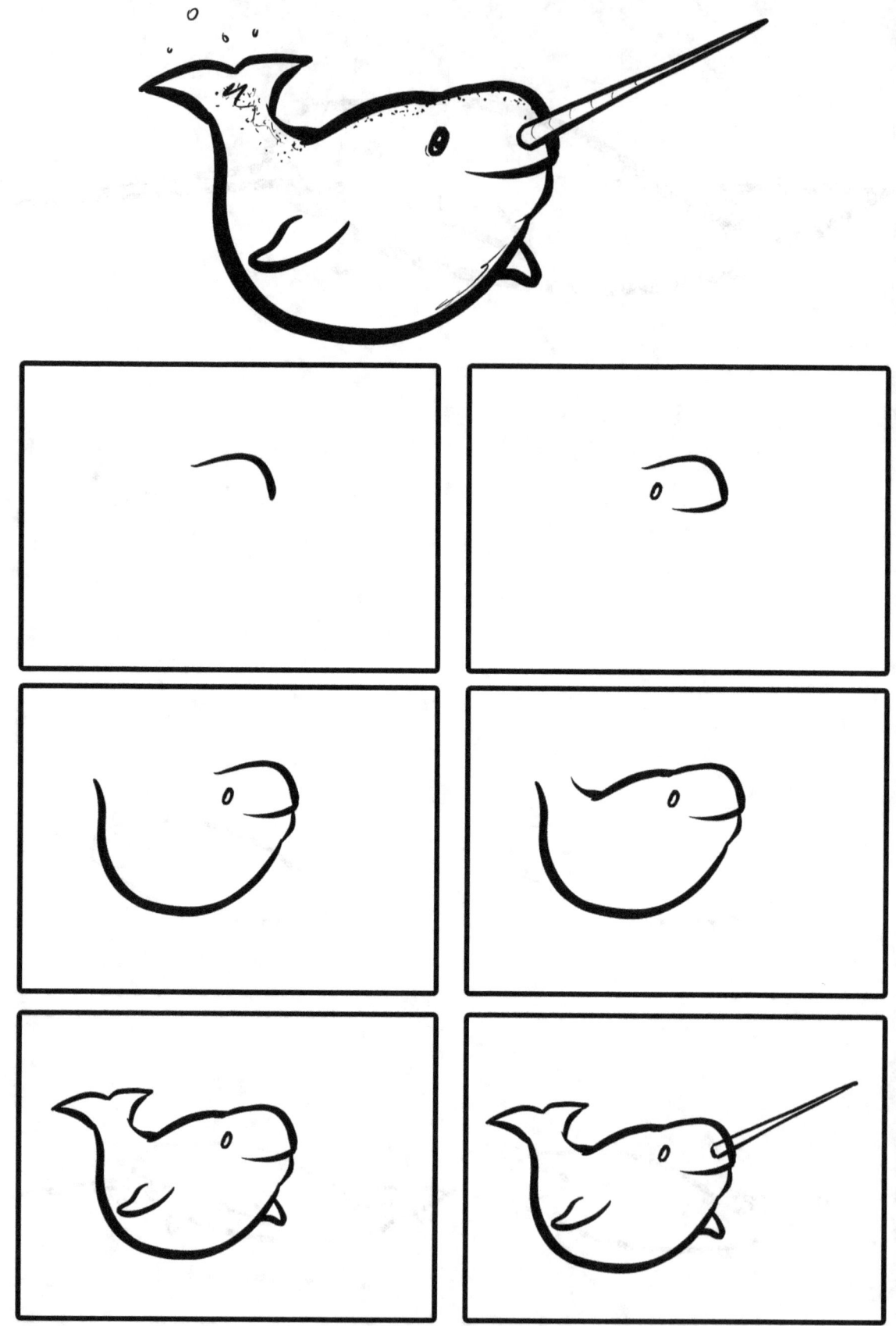

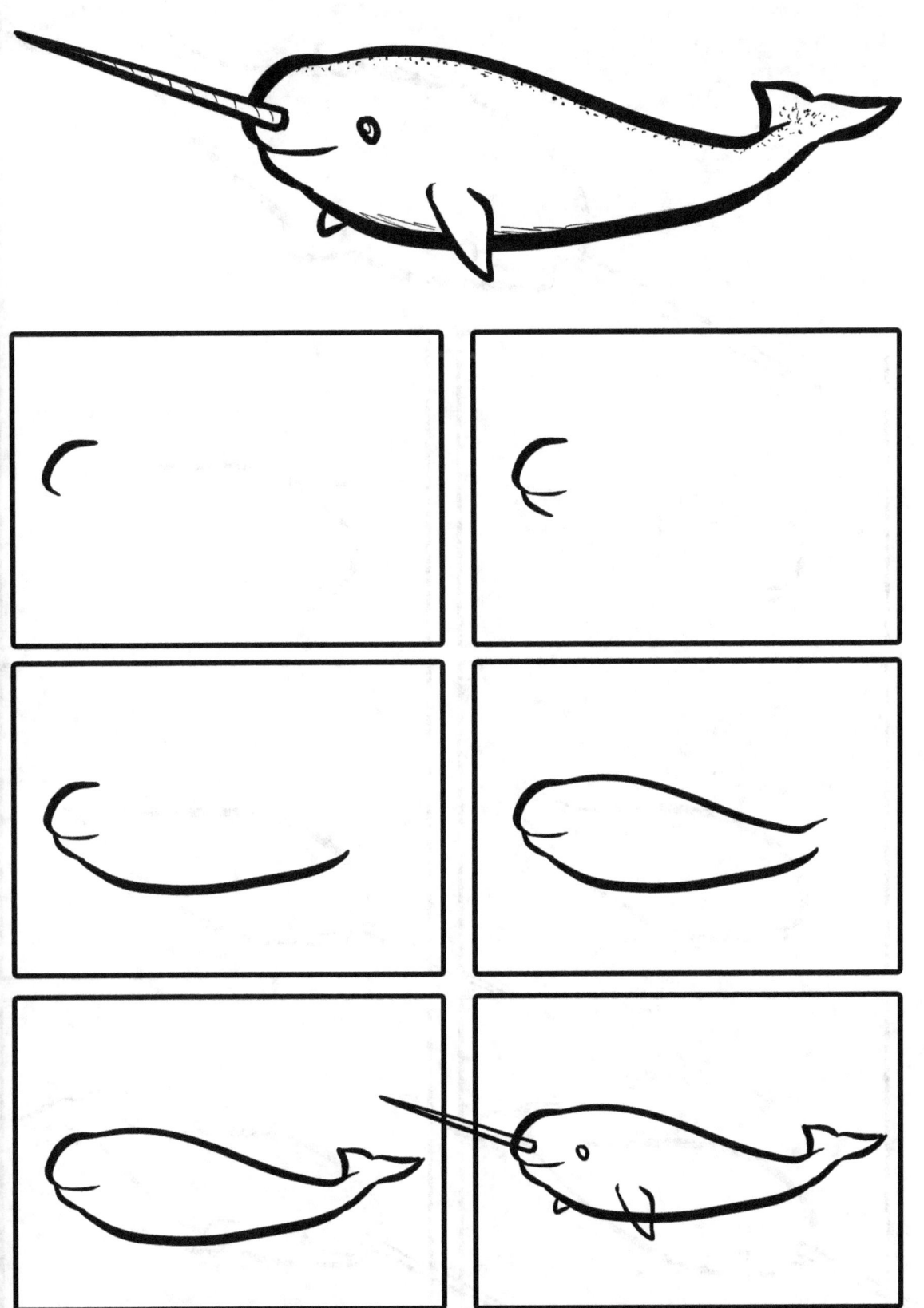

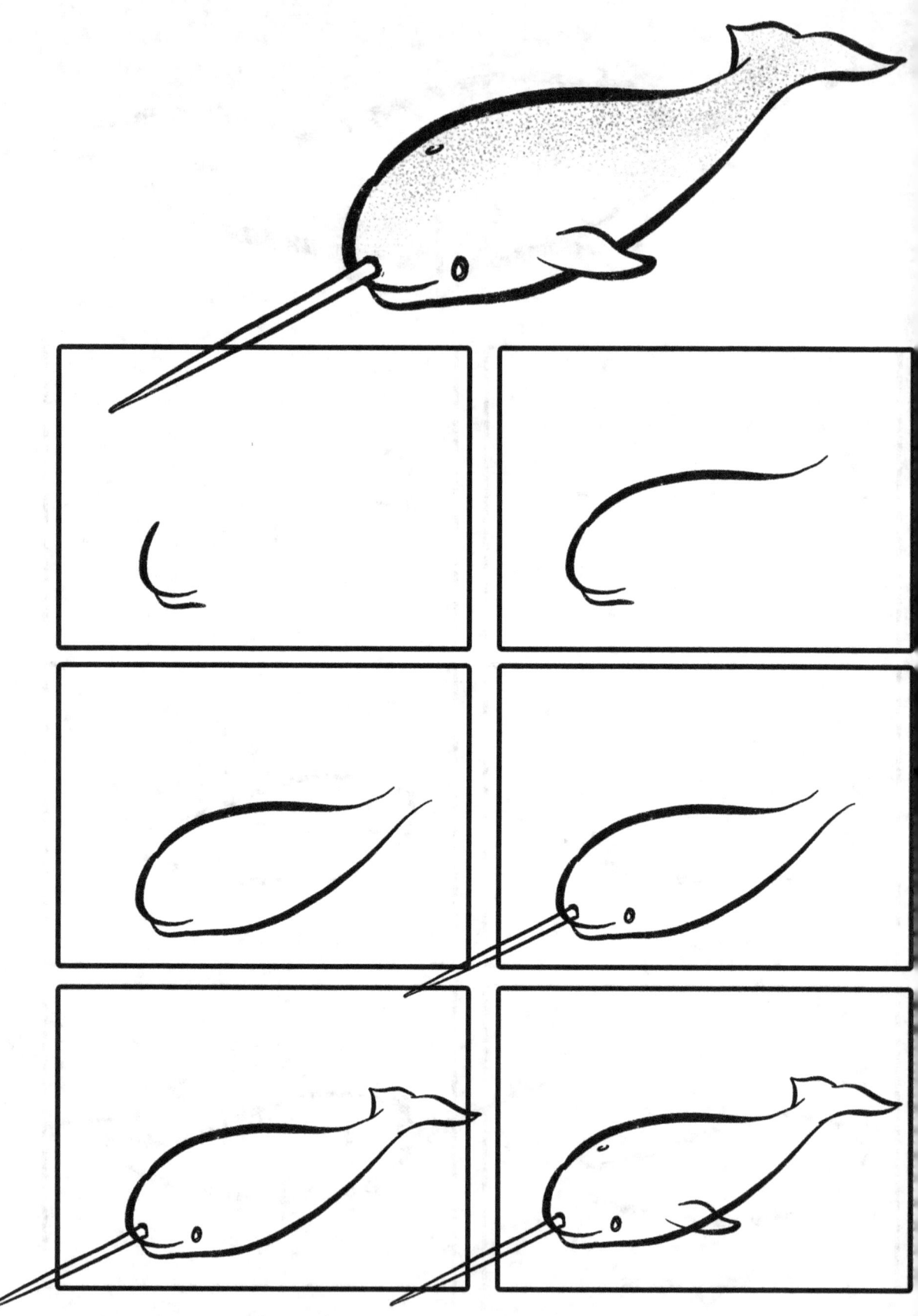

Advanced Tips!

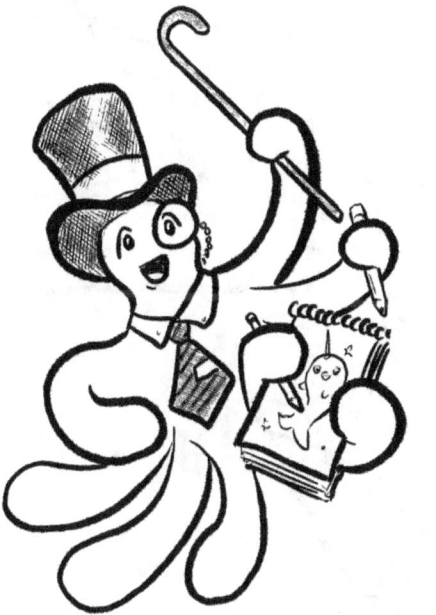

Drawing is like exercise: no matter how good you are, you won't get any better without practice.

Get out there and draw narwhals every day. Push your skills by sketching them from various viewing angles. Draw narwhals doing a variety of things.

Practice, practice, and practice some more. You'll likely draw many bad narwhals on your journey to draw good ones!

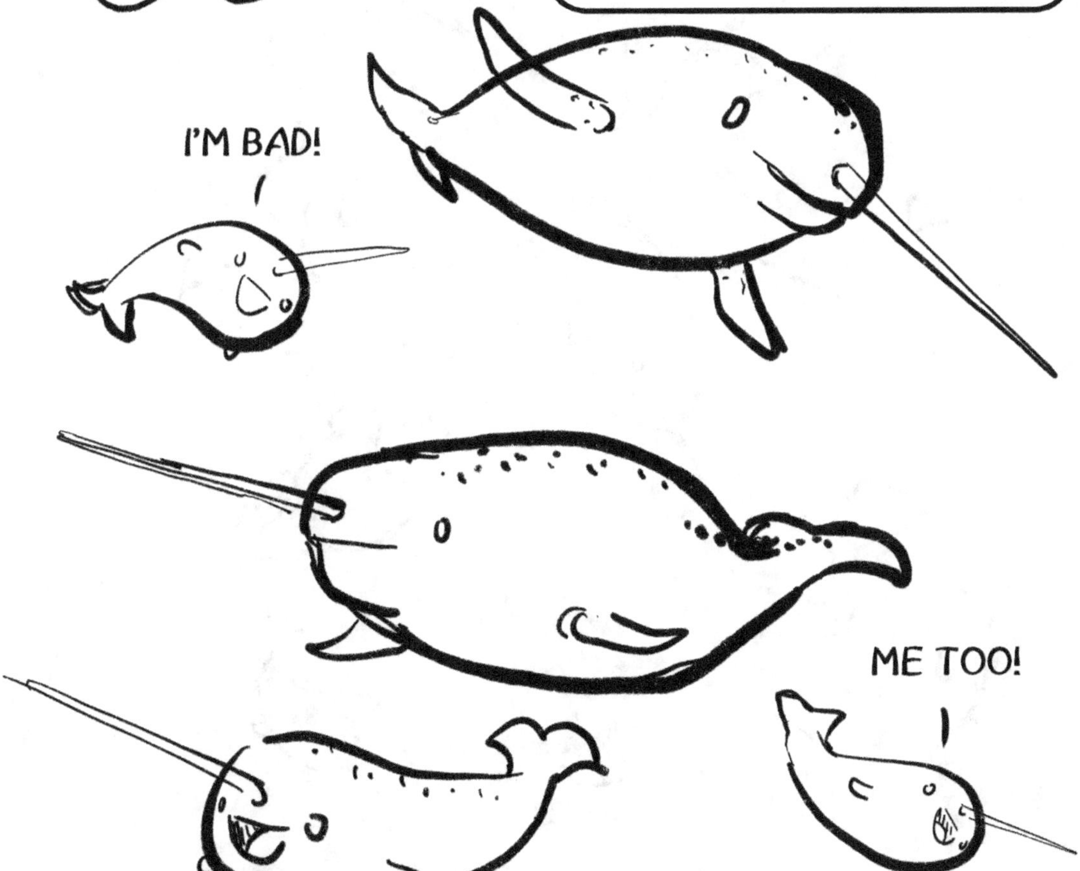

I'M BAD!

ME TOO!

One of my recommended advanced techniques is to grab a pen or pencil and sketch tiny narwhals in as few brush strokes as possible, as quickly as possible.

I find that this is a great technique to master the narwhal's form in just a few lines. Fill up a sketch pad with little narwhals for extra fun!

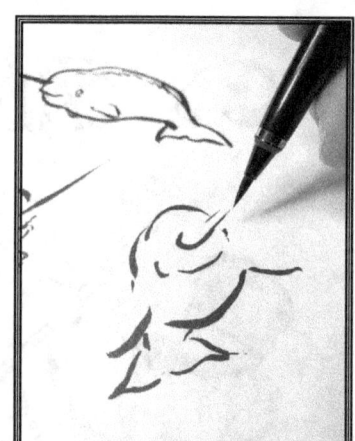

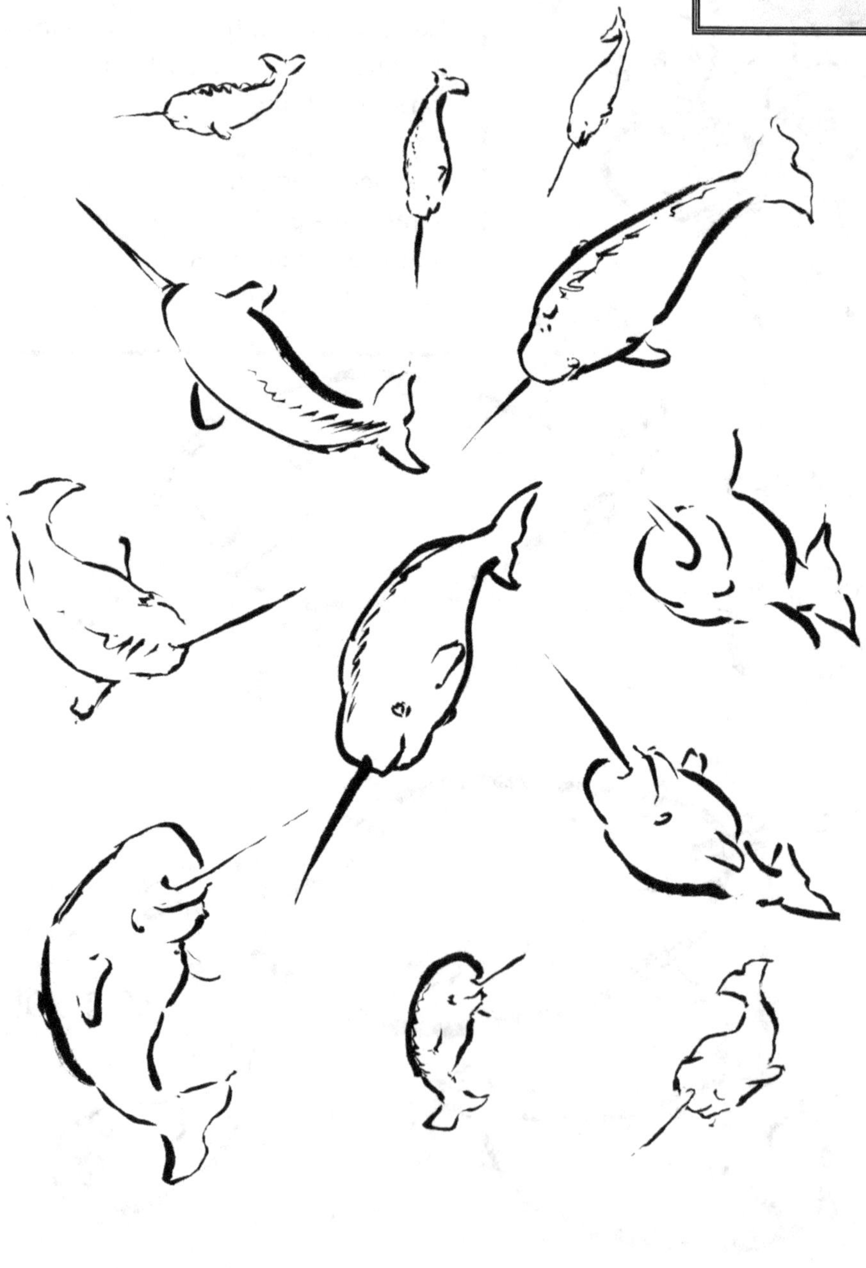

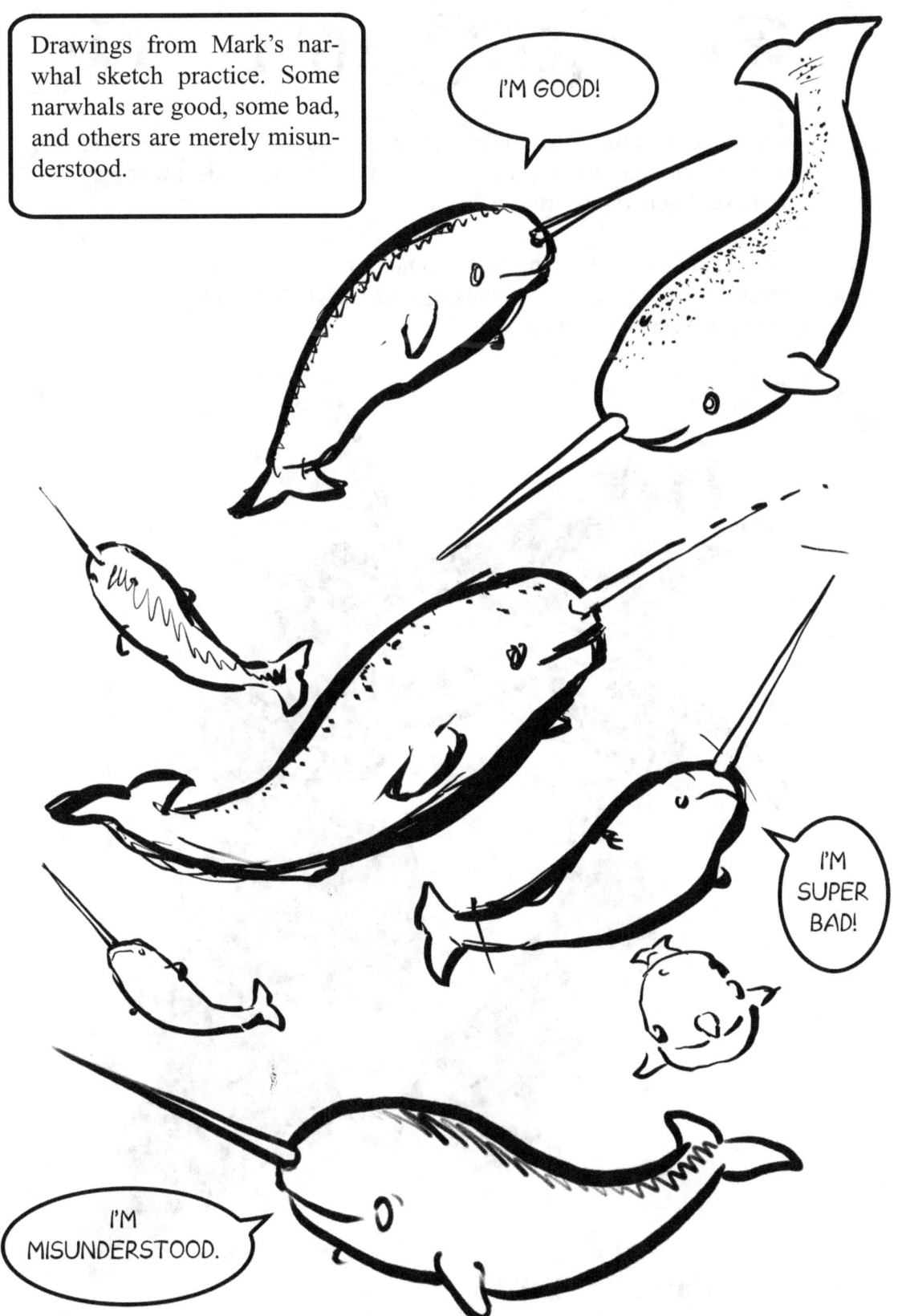

GET CREATIVE!

Now that you know how to draw narwhals, its time to let your imagination run wild. Impress your friends, family, and readers with new and exciting narwhal artwork.

Thank you for reading and enjoy some of my wacky narwhal-themed ideas! I wish you the best of luck in your narwhal-drawing adventure! May the Narwhal be with you.

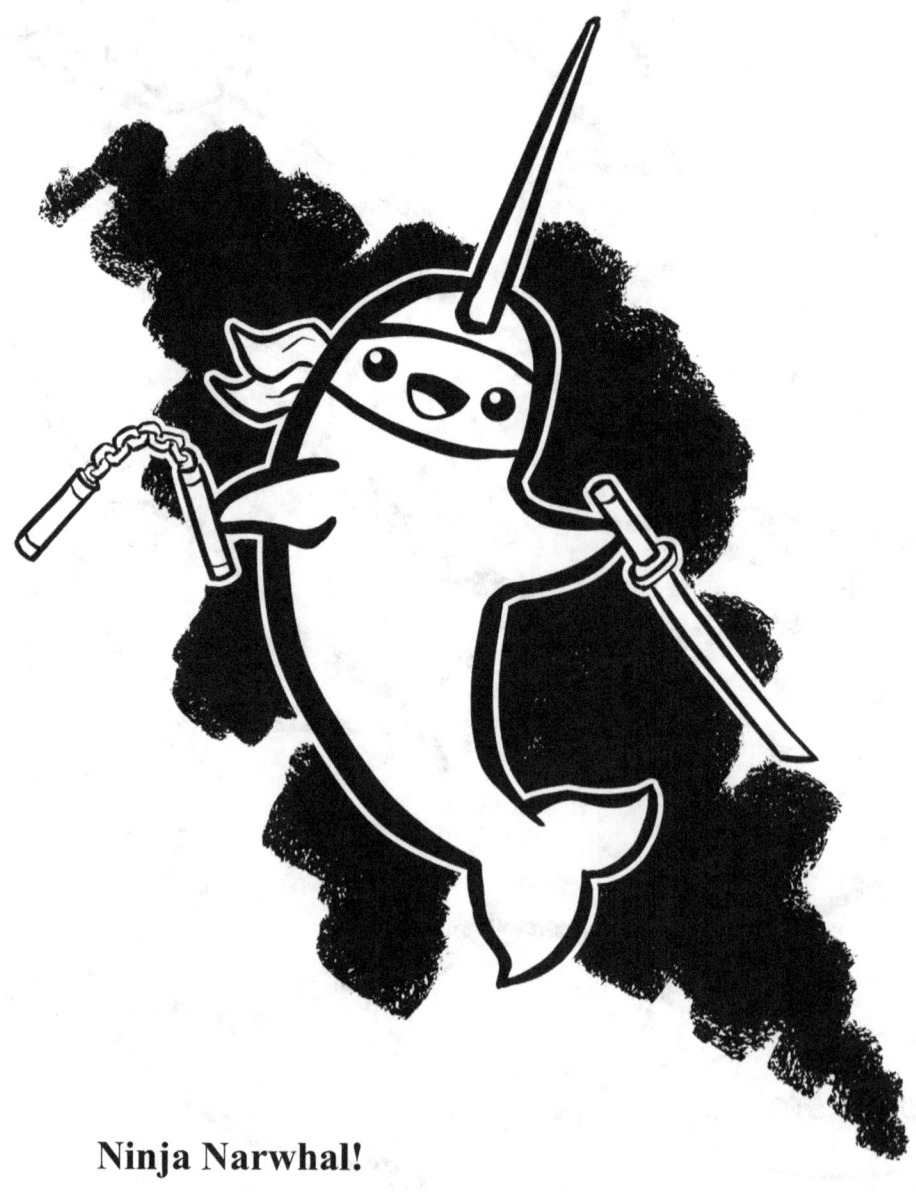

Ninja Narwhal!

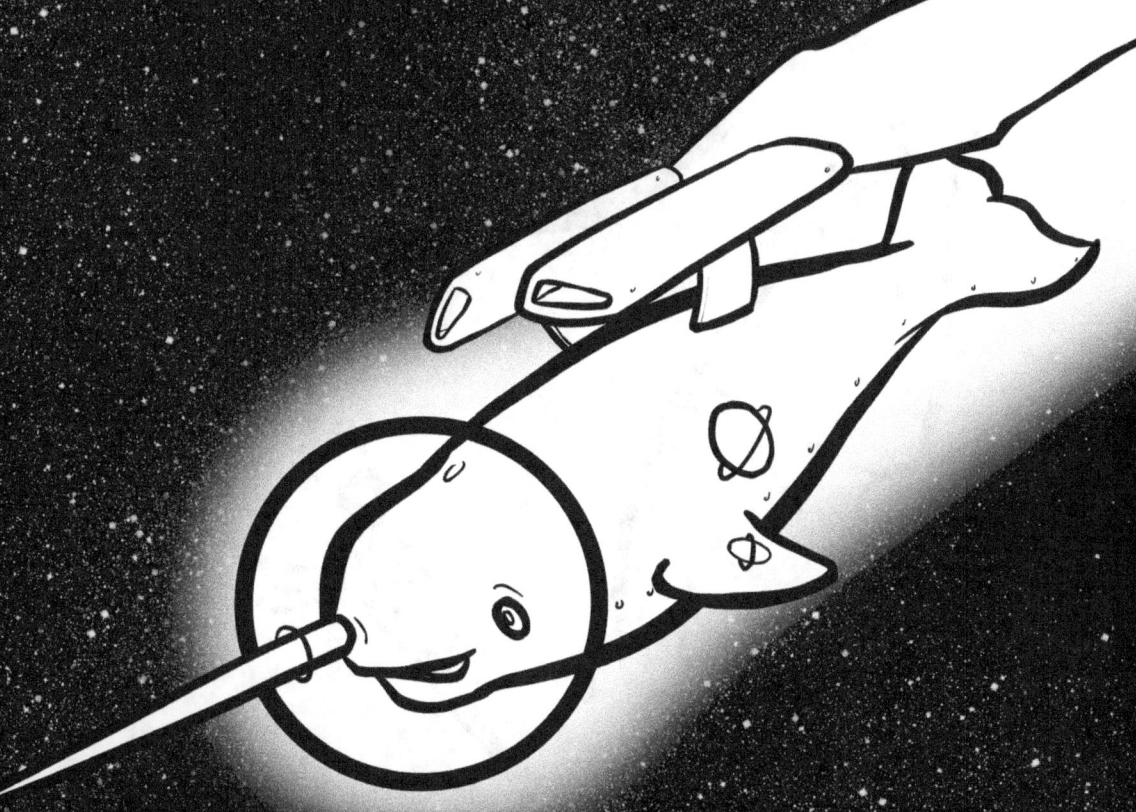

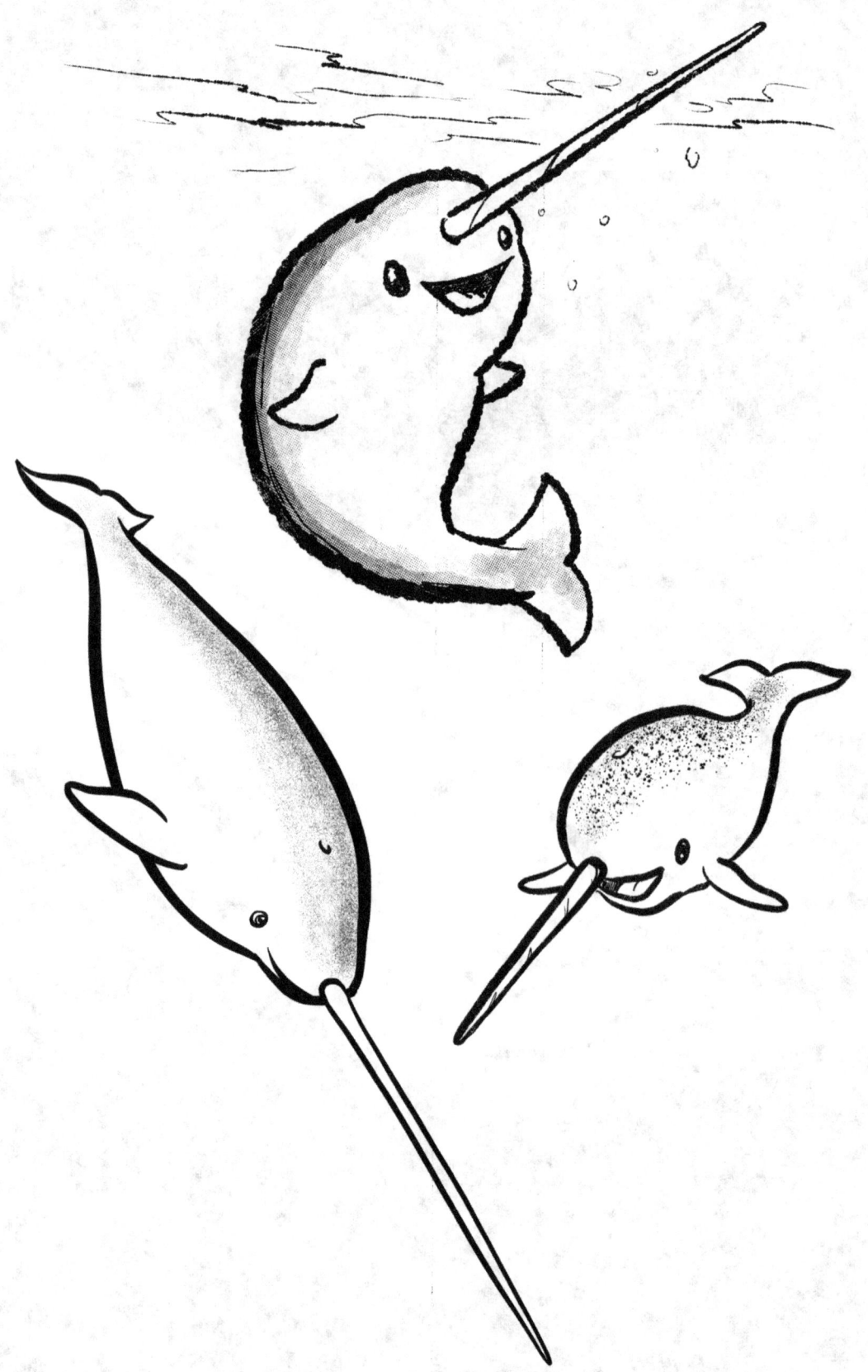

IN THE EPIC BATTLE OF
NARWHAL VS. DINOSAUR...

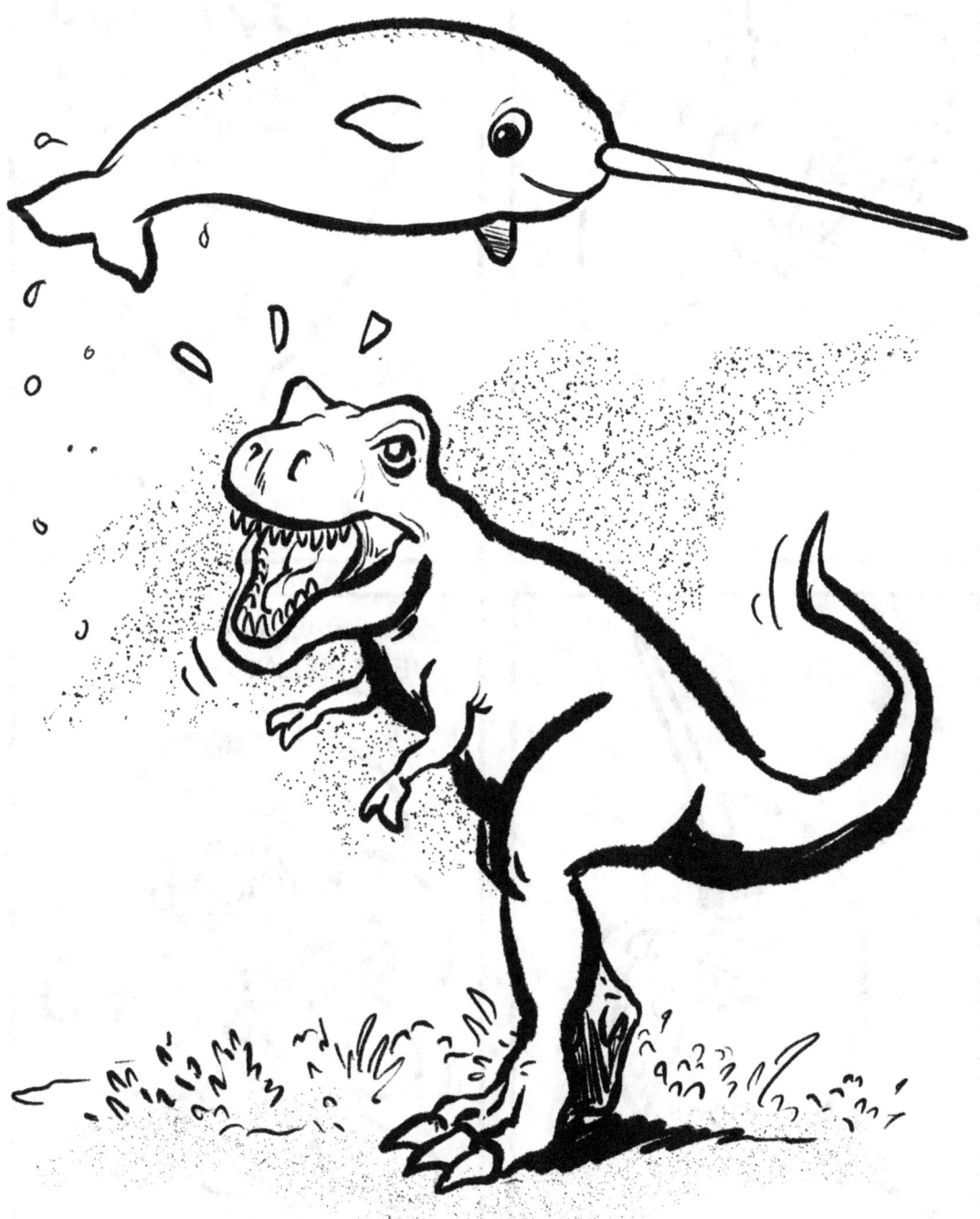

WE ALL WIN!

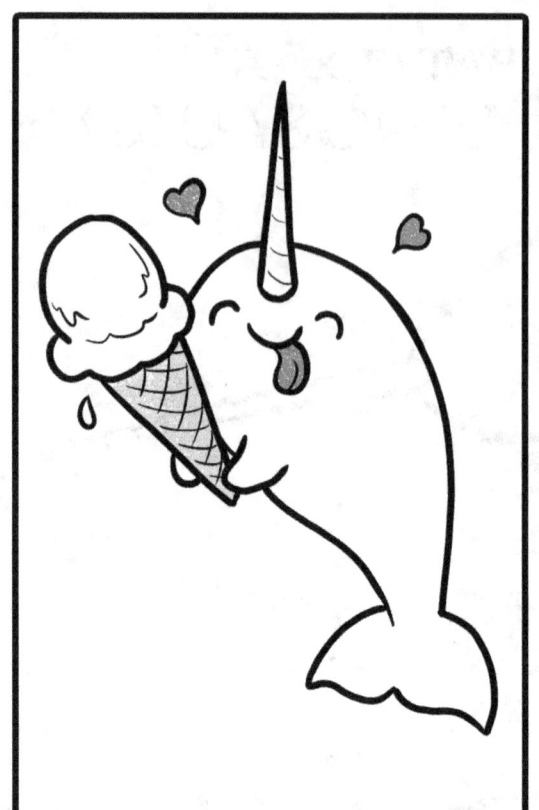
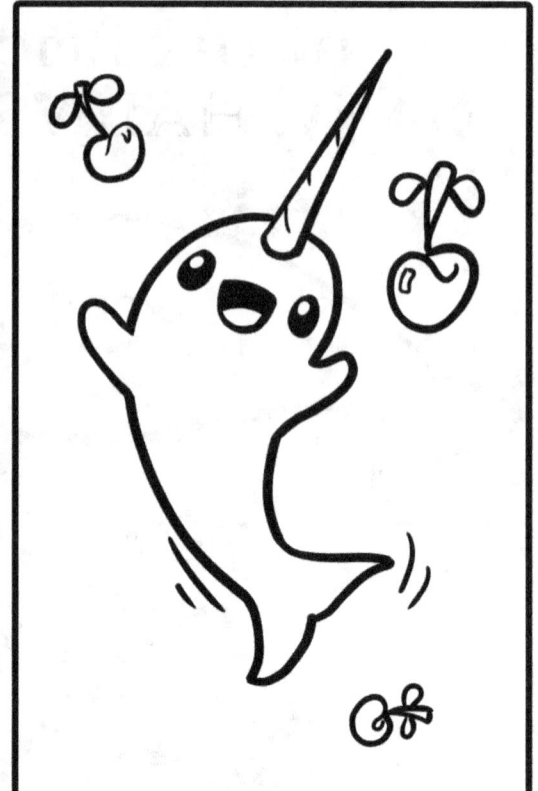
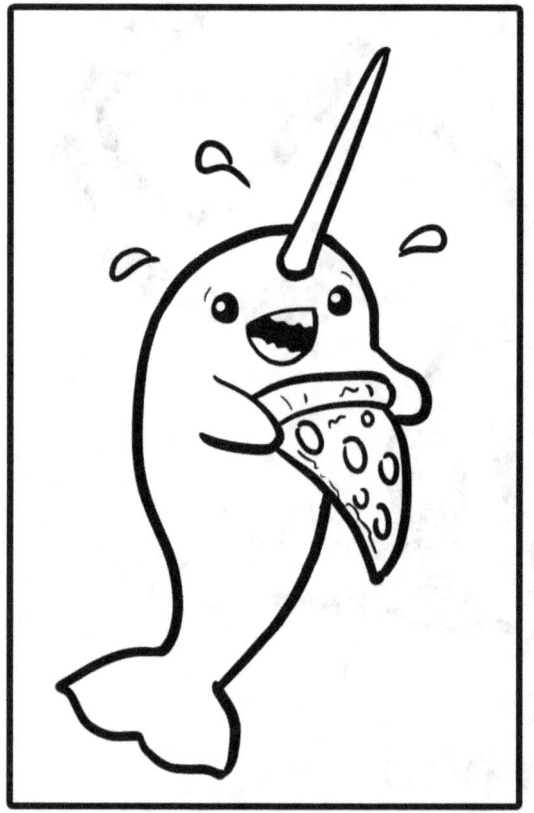
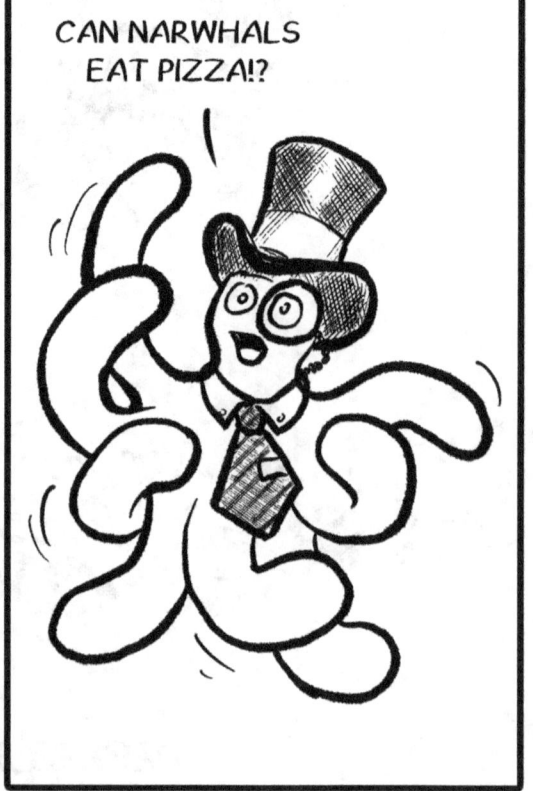

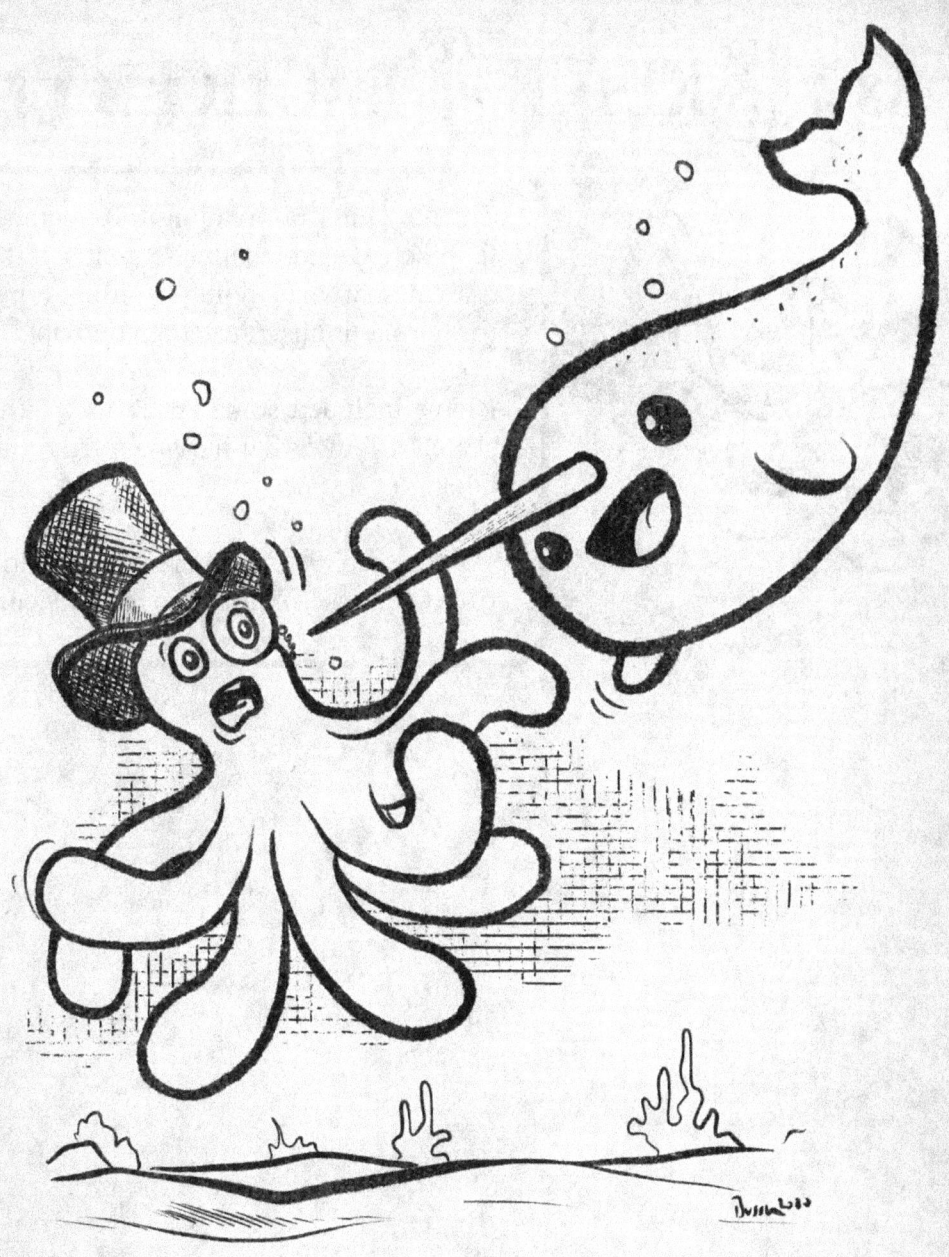

Narwhals are not horrible unless they accidentally poke you.

Sketch Practice

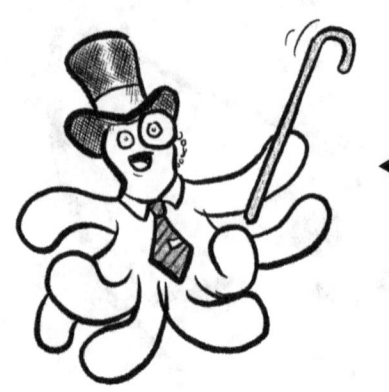

Thank you for reading! Remember to practice and challenge yourself by drawing narwhals doing exciting things (or boring things.) Just keep drawing!

I have included some space for you to sketch a few of the narwhals from this book.

You can see my adventures in The Horrible Octopus at **HorribleOctopus.com**

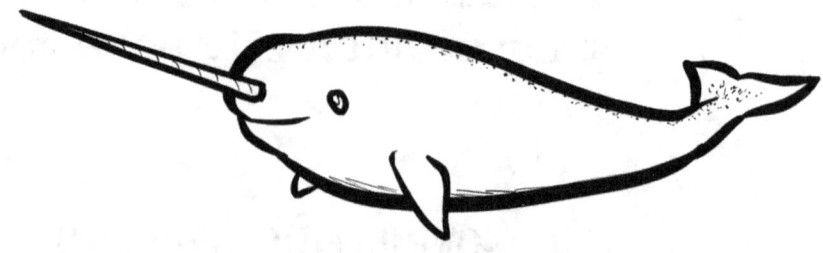

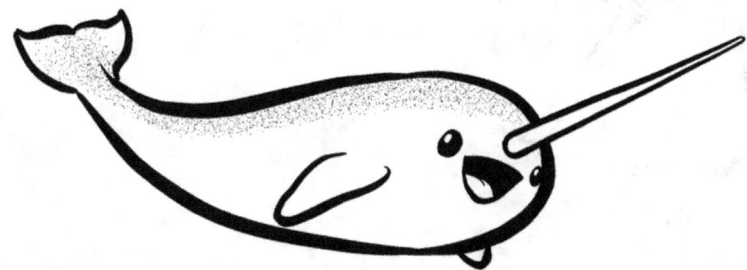

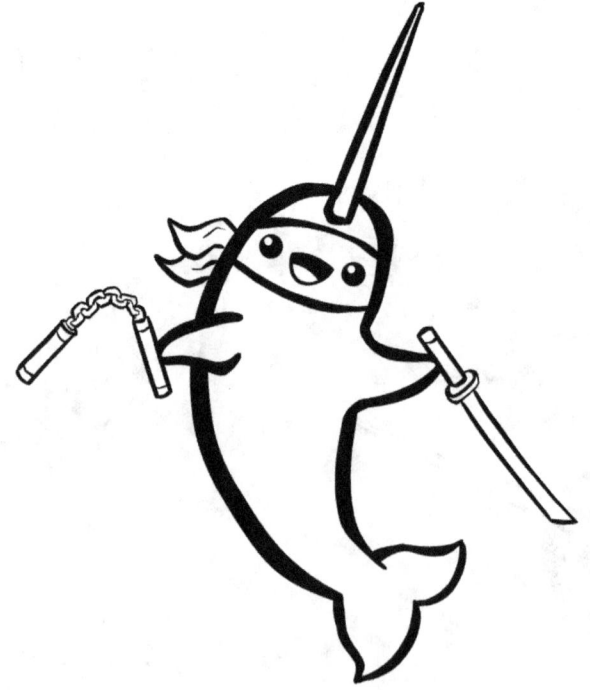

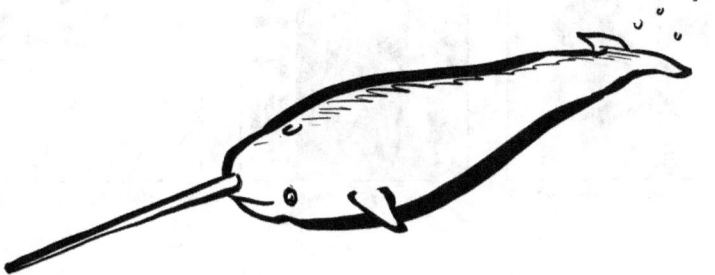

Other books from CGR Publishing at Amazon.com

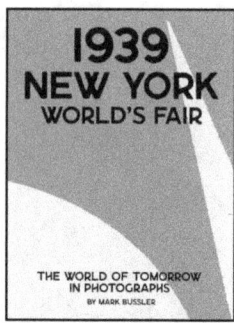
1939 New York World's Fair: The World of Tomorrow in Photographs

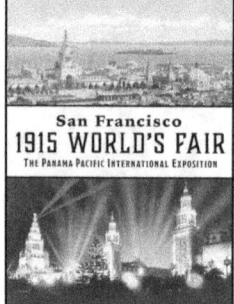
San Francisco 1915 World's Fair: The Panama-Pacific International Expo.

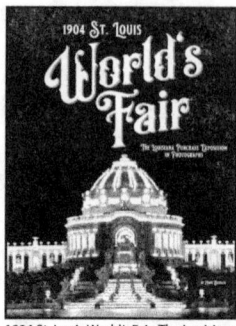
1904 St. Louis World's Fair: The Louisiana Purchase Exposition in Photographs

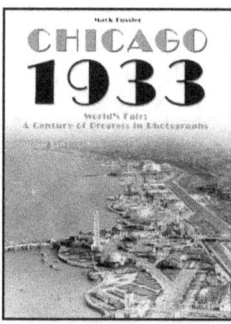
Chicago 1933 World's Fair: A Century of Progress in Photographs

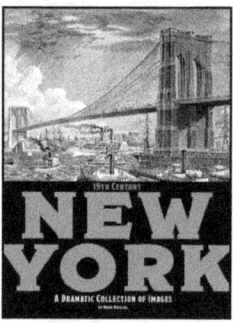
19th Century New York: A Dramatic Collection of Images

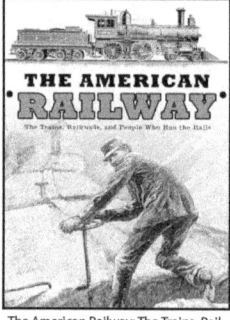
The American Railway: The Trains, Railroads, and People Who Ran the Rails

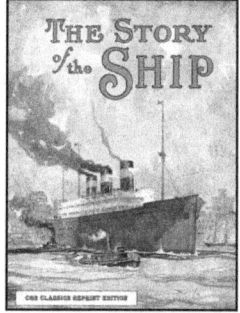
The Story of the Ship

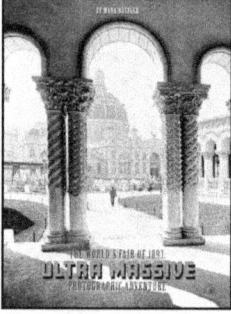
The World's Fair of 1893 Ultra Massive Photographic Adventure Vol. 1

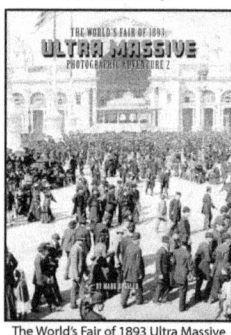
The World's Fair of 1893 Ultra Massive Photographic Adventure Vol. 2

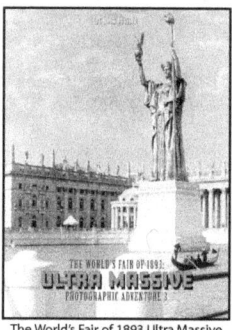
The World's Fair of 1893 Ultra Massive Photographic Adventure Vol. 3

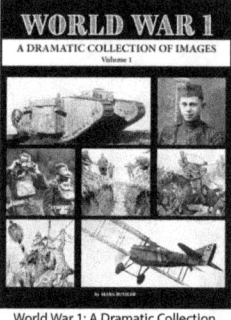
World War 1: A Dramatic Collection of Images

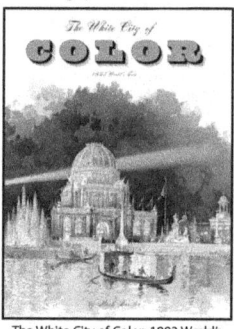
The White City of Color: 1893 World's Fair

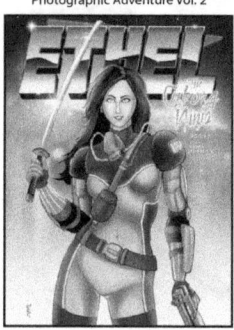
Ethel the Cyborg Ninja Book 1

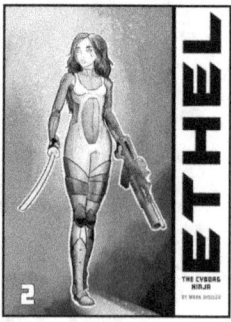
Ethel they Cyborg Ninja 2

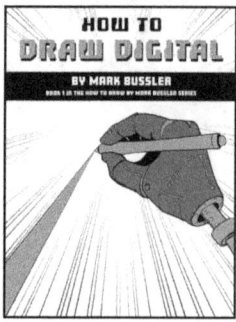
How To Draw Digital by Mark Bussler

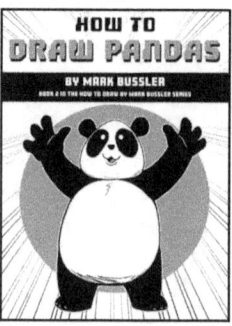
How To Draw Pandas by Mark Bussler

Other books from CGR Publishing at Amazon.com

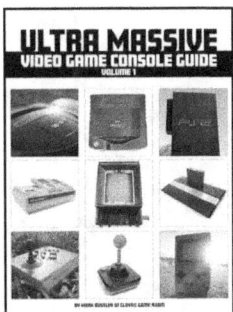
Ultra Massive Video Game Console Guide Volume 1

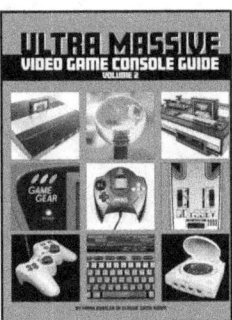
Ultra Massive Video Game Console Guide Volume 2

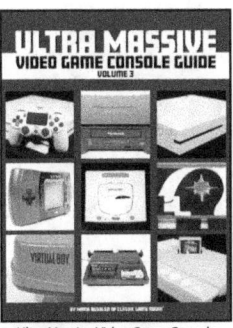
Ultra Massive Video Game Console Guide Volume 3

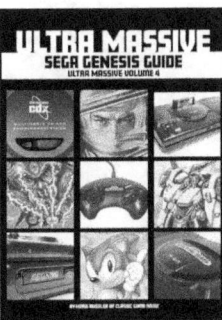
Ultra Massive Sega Genesis Guide

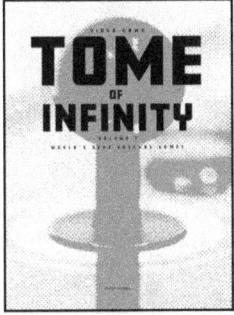
Tome of Infinity Volume 1: World's Obscure Games

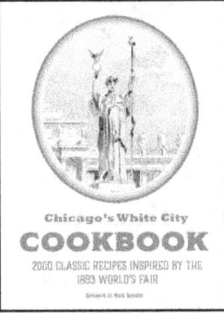
Chicago's White City Cookbook

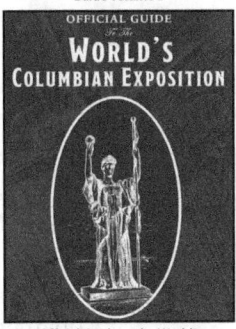
Official Guide to the World's Columbian Exposition

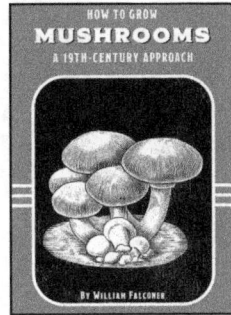
How To Grow Mushrooms: A 19th Century Approach

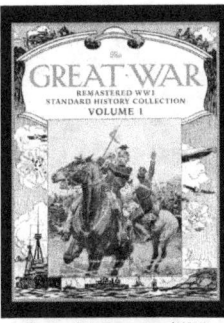
The Great War Remastered WW1 Standard History Collection Vol. 1

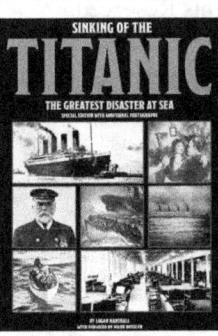
Sinking of the Titanic: The Greatest Disaster at Sea

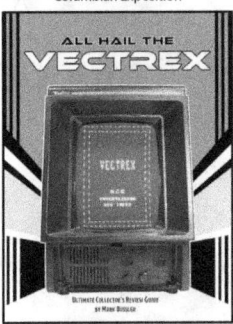
All Hail the Vectrex Ultimate Collector's Guide

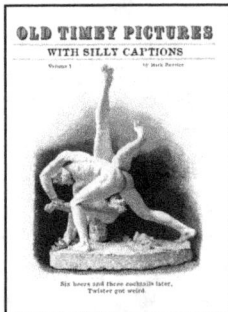
Old Timey Pictures with Silly Captions Volume 1

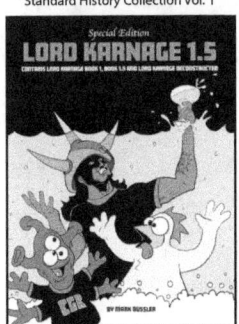
Lord Karnage 1.5

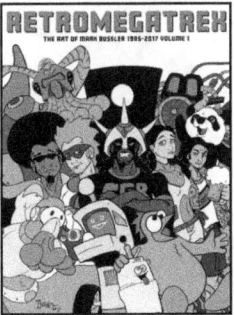
Retromegatrex: The Art of Mark Bussler 1995-2017

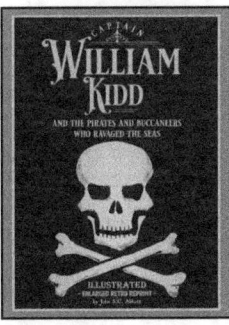
Captain William Kidd and the Pirates and Buccaneers Who Ravaged the Seas

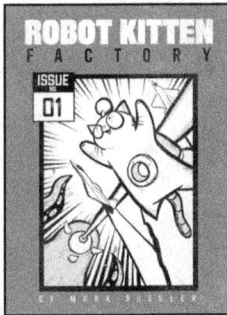
Robot Kitten Factory Issue #1

HOW TO DRAW NARWHALS
by Mark Bussler

Copyright © 2020 Inecom, LLC.
All Rights Reserved

www.CGRpublishing.com

www.ingramcontent.com/pod-product-compliance
Lightning Source LLC
Chambersburg PA
CBHW080528220526
45465CB00006B/2631